PAY HEED TO THE PROPHECIES OF NOSTRADAMUS

THE THIRD ANTICHRIST . . .
Mabus will soon die and there will come a terrible defeat for people and animals: then suddenly one will seek vengeance, thirst, hunger when the comet will run.

THE GREAT FAMINE
The great famine that I sense coming, often changing, and then becoming global will be so great and long that people will take roots from the ground, and children from the breast.

THE GLOBAL CLIMATE CRISIS
For forty years the rainbow will not appear, for forty more it will be seen each day, the parched earth will again become dry, and then great floods will return once again.

THE NEW WORLD ORDER
One day the great powers will become friends, and their power will increase. America will be at the height of its power. To the man of blood the opportunity will be given . . .

The two will not remain united long, and in thirteen years they will surrender to the Middle East. There will be much loss on both sides, and Pope Peter will be needed . . .

D0200066

NOSTRADAMUS

2003–2025

A HISTORY OF THE FUTURE

PETER LORIE

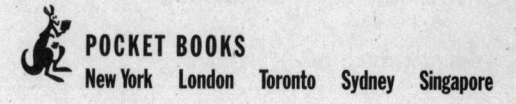

POCKET BOOKS
New York   London   Toronto   Sydney   Singapore

An *Original* Publication of POCKET BOOKS

 POCKET BOOKS, a division of Simon & Schuster, Inc.
1230 Avenue of the Americas, New York, NY 10020

ISBN: 0-7434-5339-5

First Pocket Books trade paperback printing October 2002

10 9 8 7 6 5 4 3 2 1

POCKET and colophon are registered trademarks of Simon & Schuster, Inc.

For information regarding special discounts for bulk purchases, please contact Simon & Schuster Special Sales at 1-800-456-6798 or business@simonandschuster.com

Printed in the U.S.A.

CONTENTS

INTRODUCTION

*The future is not some place we are going to, but one
    we are creating.
The paths are not to be found, but made, and the
    activity of making them
changes both the maker and the destination.*
                —*John Schaar*[1]

The Practical Nostradamus

This book combines future expectations for the early years of
this millennium, integrating the prophecies from Nostradamus's,
famous ten-volume work the *Centuries*, with visions offered by
modern authors and scientists, economy experts, and journal-
ists.[2] The idea is to create a book that explores the sixteenth-
century prophet's extraordinary ability to see far into his future
and at the same time to exemplify the future envisioned by contemporary individuals, many of whom have spent years mapping
trends that are likely to occur in what is now an immediate
future through the early part of this century. What we find in this
prophetic partnership is a remarkable synchronicity.

    Michel de Nostradame was born at the beginning of the

1

sixteenth century into a Jewish family in France. His family was forced to convert to Roman Catholicism because of the threat of the Spanish Inquisition, a powerful, militant delegation of the Holy Roman Church that roamed Southern Europe rooting out what the Church believed to be anti-Christian behavior. This was defined so as to include the work of witches in the rural areas of a world that still functioned on a pagan foundation, albeit more than a thousand years after the birth of the Christian faith. Some would say, probably correctly, that this "cleansing" was nothing more than prejudice against women, because for the most part it was women who passed the Wicca magic from one generation to the next. But there was also a great deal of occult practice among men, who still secretly studied alchemy, the occult, and astrology—the three cornerstones of ancient belief. Nostradamus was to become one of the most famous of these practitioners.

Nostradamus was carefully educated in the arts of the occult and provided with all the Judaic background to his true faith as he was brought to adulthood by two loving relatives, his uncle and grandfather, who also encouraged him into the medical profession. He grew up to be a brilliant and innovative doctor, living at a time when the bubonic plague was blitzing Europe, especially in France, where Nostradamus lived, and in Italy, where he spent much of his life. Dr. de Nostradame studied the ancient natural cures and introduced them to his contemporaries in France. He used, for example, crushed and dried flower petals and oils. These provided vitamin C and other health-giving properties to the suffering, who might otherwise have been subjected to "bleeding" by doctors who typically appeared on the doorstep of a patient's home with a necklace of garlic around their neck and pieces of garlic stuffed up their noses in a vain ploy to prevent the ghastly plague from spreading. Even the young Dr. de Nostradame recognized the foolishness of these bizarre attempts at medicine, and successfully reverted to the pagan cures used by the Wicca tradition for thousands of years.

Though there are stories of how Nostradamus discovered his rather special gift even at an early age in small events such as predicting birth dates and the sex of unborn children. In adulthood, he focused instead on his medical practice, curing thousands of plague victims in his hometown and beyond. He was also, however, a skilled and successful astrologer, so much so that his work came to the attention of the French royal family. Catherine de' Medici, King Henry II's queen, was a politically powerful woman with strong interests in the occult, which she hid behind a Roman Catholic public persona. She summoned the astrologer to Paris, providing transportation for him on a journey that took more than a month (a journey Nostradamus complains about vociferously in his writings). He brought his astrological ephemeras to read the charts of the court nobles, his perfumes and cosmetics to bring youth to their skins, and he made one of his most famous prophecies, that Henry II would die in a so-called fake jousting tournament. The prophecy was, needless to say, not at all popular with the king, but Catherine was so taken by this enigmatic prophet that she adopted him as her unofficial adviser in matters of the future. The death of Henry occurred almost exactly when Nostradamus predicted, four years later, and under the precise circumstances he had described: with a splinter from a spear to his eye through his jousting helmet. This, of itself, established Nostradamus as the world's greatest living prophet of the time.

Nostradamus's Methods

Nostradamus's most important written reference for the methods of the magical aspect of his work was a Latin translation, published in Venice in 1497 by Marsilio Ficino, of a book by a fourth-century philosopher named Jamblichus.[3] In his book, compiled a thousand years before Nostradamus lived as a documentation of all the magic of the ancient world, Jamblichus provided rituals, devices, potions, methods, and all manner of secrets. His goal was to save the rituals and devices of the ancient world against the impending Christian era, which the author feared, with good reason, would attempt to drown pagan practice.

An edition of Ficino's translation of Jamblichus was published in Lyons, close to Nostradamus's home in Salon, in 1549, at the time when the prophet was scribbling his prophetic verses in the middle of each night. (Documentation left behind by Nostradamus's son, César, and his helper, Chavigny, contends that the original prophecies were scribbled on pieces of paper during trance sessions, mostly in the middle of the night and with the help of occult magic and large quantities of nutmeg, which affects the body and mind in a way similar to modern ecstasy drugs—though the quantities of nutmeg required were ingested over long periods of time and in very large amounts.) Nostradamus's methods of using water gazing, trance, and other rituals are precisely documented in the *Centuries*, the opening verses of which are almost literal French versions of Ficino's Latin translation of Jamblichus.

The following morning the scribbled prophecies would be gathered up and transcribed into legible script by Nostradamus's helpers. Nostradamus would then "fix" them in time and space, using what was considered to be the *science* of astrology for the temporal aspects. His visions were literally pictures of the future, and needed to be organized somehow in the sober light of day, his precise knowledge of the future positions of the planets serving to provide this requirement. The end result, a series of extensive notes and commentaries, was then turned into the verses, or quatrains, written in French, Latin, and other languages to disguise their content. These verses were arranged in chronological order at that point, dating from Nostradamus's lifetime on to 3797, the year he tells us the planet Earth will die or cease to contain human life.

The last step was to jumble the verses out of temporal sequence and organize them into the order in which they appear in the *Centuries*. This was done to prevent the Roman Catholic Church authorities of the time from comprehending the prophet's work, thus avoiding the Spanish Inquisition, he hoped. Nostradamus was as much at risk from militant Church authorities as any witch.

In the coming pages of this book, for each event in each year or series of years, the English translation of the original is provided with the interpretation. To confuse the authorities of his time, Nostradamus deliberately clouded his work in obscurity, using prophetic language, anagrams, complex and hidden dating methods, astrology, obscure names and locations, and arcane terminology. This has been taken into account in the translation and interpretation of the verses.

It is not that Nostradamus did not want us to understand him, for his whole philosophy was that if we could see the future, we could alter it beneficially. But the whole tradition of magical and mystical understanding was intrinsically inhibited by the need to work hard in order to succeed. The doctrines of ancient alchemy exemplify this tradition. If it wasn't enormously difficult, then it wasn't enormously useful. Even the relatively young Christian religions are filled with astrological and alchemical references borrowed from much older religious doctrines and beliefs—mystical traditions that influenced Nostradamus more profoundly than Catholicism. As mentioned above, Nostradamus was Jewish by birth and studied the ancient Cabalistic understanding of God, which still contained a good deal of alchemy and other pagan rituals as a major part of its doctrines. The basis of what we might call mystical camouflage is that the essence is shrouded in mystery, indeed, ultimately unknowable. But we can dig into these depths and be rewarded if we understand the smoke and mirrors employed. And although you will not be asked to comprehend all this bizarre camouflaging, it is of interest to learn something of how it works.

Decoding the Prophet

1. *Anagrams.* One of Nostradamus's favorite methods of disguising his prophecies is through the use of anagrams, in

which he scrambles words like crossword clues. Henry II becomes "chyren," which, when unscrambled, becomes "Henryc," the Latin version of the name. Colonel Khaddafi is "Adaluncatif," which we can turn into "Catafi Luna," or Khaddafi of the Crescent Moon (the crescent of Islam).

2. *Obscure names and locations.* In one of his most famous verses, Nostradamus refers to a place called "Angoulmois," a location in the France of his time, in relation to the date July 1999, which is specifically mentioned in the same verse. The area is also known as Angouléme, and during Nostradamus's lifetime the Count of Angouléme was also King Francis I (the king who followed Henry II). A man in Francis's court, Giovanni da Verrazano, was sent by his king to discover new lands across the oceans, and landed, during his travels, on an island off the coast of what would become America. This was very close to the time when Columbus landed on the mainland of America. Verrazano named this island Angouléme, after his king. It later became Manhattan Island (Manhattanites will be familiar with the Verrazano Bridge). This kind of extraordinary, complex, and yet fascinating wordplay is common to the verses.

3. *Dating methods.* Each verse, or quatrain, is numbered. There are ten groups of quatrains, known as "centuries," and each verse is numbered within that "century." This is how Nostradamus arranged his verses after jumbling them up at random, and so we find Century 1, Verse 10, designated as C1 V10. But, as always with this enigmatic prophet, the story is not as simple as that. Occasionally the date of successful predictions coincides with the cen-

tury and verse numbers. We cannot say that this dating method works very often, but it can help in the detective hunt when combined with other evidence in the verse, along with the actual dates and astrological clues. We cannot suppose that even Nostradamus was able to date precisely every event he foresaw. The use of the word *century* to describe each "chapter" of his verses does not, unfortunately, often help us to date the century in which the prediction was intended to fall. This would be all too convenient. His prophetic attempts are scattered throughout almost a thousand verses, sometimes with more than one event in a verse, and sometimes spread apart by several hundred years, which means a lot of searching and decoding is needed to find any kind of certainty. Nevertheless, the verse numbers occasionally prove helpful if we compare the contents of the prediction with current expectations.

Ordering the Verses

The basis of the ordering of dates in this short study of Nostradamus's work arises largely out of an attempt to put at least some of the verses back into the temporal order in which they originally occurred. A few verses remained in sequence, quite obviously, as the events clearly tend to follow one another. But some 90 percent of the verses were out of temporal sequence. The task of gathering verses into a sequence that appears to work is ongoing, and could not be completed for all of the verses. Further volumes may follow, and further temporally sequenced verses will emerge for any future titles. For now, however, the time line appears to work well, fixing events in the years specified.

Our Part in the Future

This book is not only about Nostradamus and his prophetic capabilities, it is also about us, the human race on earth, and our capabilities. Nostradamus saw—very often with remarkable accuracy—a future, at the turn of the twentieth and twenty-first centuries, that looked to him exactly like an apocalypse. Filled with world war scenarios; massive and wide-ranging earthquakes, floods, and other natural catastrophes; political problems; and economic fluctuations, the twentieth century would have appeared to him like no other time in history. In essence, he describes this period and the early years of this century in a way reminiscent of the biblical apocalypse from The Book of Revelation[4]—one of the other most extraordinary forms of prophetic literature—with a world that seems to be going insane prior to what the Bible describes as a time of peace and tranquillity . . . the storm before the still.

The twenty-first century, in Nostradamus's view, marks the beginning of a thousand years of peace. From this perspective, we might be forgiven for viewing the end of the twentieth century as a little like a madhouse, chaotic and apocalyptic. There was a sense in that century that much of life was out of control, that no one was at the helm. God had largely lost favor, presidents could not be relied upon, disease and war claimed more lives than ever before, and crime entered a state of violence and madness more serious and dangerous than at any time in the past. *This* could very easily have been the so-called

apocalypse. The prophecies from both the Bible and Nostradamus's *Centuries* both predict that at some time around
"now" a thousand years of peace would begin. These time
periods, of course, don't take their cues from calendar dates,
so that we cannot expect this glorious "everlasting" peace of
1,000 years to coincide with any millennium value, but we are
told that a new world will emerge from the old one, and perhaps, as we will see in the coming pages, we have reached the
end of the "apocalypse," though the word itself does not mean
what we tend to think it means. If we look closely at the word
"apocalypse," it breaks down into Latin as "Ap kali ipse,"
which translates into English as "from the call itself," the "call"
being the spiritual call of God to consciousness, enlighten-
ment, or awakening. This is not a physical state but a state of
the soul. The call is the call that the individual receives to
become a monk/nun or priest—a person of God. This is literally God calling us. So, from the original teachings of the Old
Testament and those of Jesus and John, the apocalypse is the
time in which spiritual death and rebirth occurs on a massive
scale. Those who receive the call become transformed and
those who don't catch the train go to hell. Perhaps the apocalyptic age we are transforming through is literally a new call to
God, and not a physical end or transformation of the world.

More significant than the sense of chaos and disaster in
the last century is the understanding that we are the sole
cause of it. No one else is to blame. This realization may be
one of the most important of all time, for if we accept our own
part—the greater part—in this scenario of world transformation, we must also accept responsibility for changing it. The
future, disasters and all, is created "man-ually." Many individu-

als in the past came to this realization on their own. Nostradamus, for one, made the point several times in his epistles and verses that there would come a time—*this* time—when mankind would become aware of his powers over his own fate and be in a position to change the future, hopefully for the better. Acceptance brings power. We are no longer able to blame nature, or political leaders, or other people's greed and foolishness. We are no longer, for the most part, controlled by distant kings and queens, or powerful autocrats and generals. We no longer even have God to blame. That leaves *us* in command. We elect the politicians. We are polluting our environment and wasting our resources. *We* created God in the first place. We are responsible, and so we can make the changes for the better—or worse.

No single individual in the history of prophecy is better known than Nostradamus. As an "engineer" of the future, living in sixteenth-century Europe, he turned what at that time was a complex, mostly muddled, and secretive art—bound up in magic and mysticism—into something more of a science. Even the biblical prophecies remain shrouded in eschatological complexity, employing language intended to remain essentially mystical (i.e., written for the "secret gathering of individuals with special knowledge"—the definition of the source word *mysterium*).[5]

But to say that Nostradamus's quatrains are written in simple language would be a gross exaggeration. Hundreds of translators and interpreters have made as many different senses of the verses over the past four centuries. The thousand or so verses have been applied to many different times and events, and as the future gathers speed before us, verses that failed to work on past events are applied to future events in the hope that this time the interpreter will be lucky and get it right! One wonders what Nostradamus actually saw when he wrote the word *Hister*, for example. Was it a river in Austria, or the "second Antichrist," Adolph Hitler?

Whichever, there is often a strong sense of excitement attached to reading the work of this prophet. Events *do* occur that appear closely related to the verses he wrote. During the mid-1980s, for instance, it seemed likely that Colonel Khaddafi of Libya might be the subject of a verse that begins, "There will be a melting of a great fleet."[6] Other references in that verse and subsequent verses, which concentrate on Middle Eastern conflicts and a certain "Colonel," inspired the author's idea that something frightening might occur shortly on the confrontational stage between the United States and the Middle East. The interpretation of these verses was completed in January 1986. Just three months later, on the twenty-fourth of March, Colonel Khaddafi declared his "Line of Death," a naval barrier not to be crossed by the U.S. fleet, which had taken up cautionary positions in the Mediterranean.[7] The excitement engendered by the recognition of an event already interpreted is so great that one begins to understand the passion and energy Nostradamus experienced after he began to cultivate his own prophetic powers.

Many stories are told of events in which Nostradamus predicted the future and then watched reality fulfill his words. Try to imagine yourself successfully achieving even a minor prediction of your own future: The result would be both enormously exciting *and* very frightening. And in that foreknowledge, what would you do differently? On a grander scale, how would world authorities—politicians, teachers, economists—change their ways if they believed in an accurate and scientific prophetic method? Would John Kennedy have died? And if he hadn't—because he had listened to the prophets who predicted his death—how would the world thereafter have been changed?

But this is all academic, for most of the world is skeptical about prophecy, because it is still shrouded so darkly in the shadows of magic and disbelief. And yet, in this millennial era, we spend a great amount of time gazing into our crystal balls, with both magic and science as our tools. The last decades of the twentieth century and the beginning of the twenty-first have seen a worldwide spiritual awakening, during which astrology, palmistry, channeling, and other even more mystical arts have formulated a plethora of methods for seeing into our personal futures. In the more precise areas of politics, economics, ecology, science, and technology, barely a day goes by without a book or magazine containing material related to the future being published. We predict changes in the value of money every second of every day in the financial futures market and we continually assess the likelihood of changes in political arenas. A number of successful professional prophets are constantly preoccupied with "knowing" how national and international conditions will develop under any given circumstance. In this sense, there are many would-be Nostradamuses. We might say that prophecy has always been an inexact science, but we employ it more energetically now than at any time in our past. And as life becomes more uncertain, more frenzied, and complex, the need to know something of our future will increase still further.

This book, which could be described as a "history of the future," is concerned with the years 2003 through 2025. With that as their focal point, the texts in the following pages make use of both the mystical, the scientific, and the political. Both Nostradamus and modern prophets of the twenty-first century attempt to bring the future closer—as if it were not close enough already! We will see what Nostradamus has to say about the Computer Generation's prediction of faster and faster organic chips. We will see how the quatrains match up with where seismologists calculate the likelihood of earthquakes around the world. We will take a look at Nostradamus's words on the subject of medical advances in the fields of aging and body parts, and we will also pay special and extensive attention to the predicted rise in the power of women in every field of life, as this is felt to be of perhaps greater significance than any other single subject. And where we hope for political and economic changes during the first quarter-century of the third millennium, we will also have Nostradamus's guidance. There are times, of course, when the ancient and the modern do not meet. This is because our prophetic attempts tend to be based securely in the present, whereas Nostradamus's were created through what he believed to be divine intervention. In the pages of this book, however, we are concerned only with the successes.

When Nostradamus lived, time somehow stretched further away, more slowly than in the twenty-first century, when time has speeded up to such an extent that we can be sure anything we imagine is going to happen twenty years from now will actually happen in ten. Nevertheless, the prophecies of Nostradamus continue to amaze us. Even if we look upon his

verses with the maximum cynicism, they still bear considerable fruit for this extraordinary time of change. Though he
was concerned with many periods of the history of the future,
one of the most important was the end of what he called the
"sixth millennium" (referring to the Jewish calendar reckon-
ing) and the beginning of the "seventh" (which is the Christian
"third" millennium). More of his verses are concerned with
this time than with almost any other, perhaps with the excep-
tion of the France of his own period. It is for our own era,
however, that he actually provided real dates for events he
foresaw. For "1999 and seven months," for instance, he predicted the event in the United States that is the precursor of a
series of prophecies in this book that actually began in September 2001 (I think it is fair to give Nostradamus a leeway of
one year!).[8]

It is during this century that he also saw an apocalypse—
something most of us have feared—which might, without an
increase in human consciousness, result in the end of the
world. He warned of a third Antichrist and an increase in
earthquakes, volcanoes, and other earth-shattering events. He
foresaw political changes that we might not have imagined
possible just a few years ago—friendship between the United
States and China, for example, and the fall of Communism. He
even wrote: ". . . if the kingdoms, sects and religions were to
see the future kingdoms, sects and religions, and see how dia-
metrically opposed they are to their favorite dreams, they
would condemn what the future will know to be true . . ."[9]

In general, humans are not successful long-term prophets.
We may attempt the task of becoming Nostradamuses, but we
rarely succeed, except in the very short term, and then not so

often. So the master remains popular. Nostradamus's prophecies have stayed in print, in fact, during the entire four and a half centuries since his death. And sadly, as we open this new millennium, the gifts of prophecy become more desirable, more essential, to our lives but not necessarily more successful. Back to the drawing board. Back to Nostradamus, perhaps, for he understood our need to project our hopes onto the shadows of the future, and our tendency to overcome skepticism by imposing order on obscurity. But this only works for us in terms of Nostradamus because sometimes he gets it right—more often, in fact, than chance would allow. Who better to rely upon, therefore? In truth, hardly anybody else from the past gives us a glimmer of the future so successfully.

The actual interpretations of the future prophecies begin with the year 2003, early in the third millennium after Christ, but prior to that we have included something remarkable to show just how close Nostradamus could get to actual dates of events. This coming short section is directly related to September 11, 2001.

SEPTEMBER 11, 2001

The year 1999 and seven months, from the skies will come a great and frightening king, to devastate the great King of Angoulmois, before After Mars to reign through happiness.

—*C10 V72*[1]

This quatrain has most often been interpreted as meaning that the world was somehow going to end. It is one of the very few verses that contains an actual date in Nostradamus's future, and the year 1999 is, of course, a very emotive year as it is the end of a century and millennium (at least as far as popular belief is concerned), and could therefore be the end of an era, or even of mankind. Though, of course, it was not. The concept of a "doomsday" is popular among many interpreters. But the universe tends not to be aware of mankind's calendars, only mankind is aware of the time of day and the date of the year. Nostradamus was not a fool and would not have made such a presumption. This does not detract, however, from the importance of the whole concept of "the millennium" as a turning point in human transformation. And if we take into account the fact that Nostradamus was often wrong on his dates by a year or two (pretty good over a 450-year-long sight), we can easily apply this quatrain to September 11, 2001.

The first, most important part of this verse is the reference to "Angoulmois," for this brings us back to our suggestion that many of the prophet's verses contain words that are essentially historically sourced. Most interpreters take the name "Angoulmois" in relation only to its ancient position in the Dark Ages, so this is where we will begin our hunt.

The people of Angouleme were invaded by the Huns, a Mongol race led by a violent and powerful king named Attila. The area of Angoulmois, which was then the province of France in which the city of Angouleme stood, was a large area of southwest France now known as Charente. The city lies upon a high plateau above the conjunction of the Charente and Anguienne rivers and was therefore a great vantage point for conquering Visigoths, Huns, and Mongols. But why are we looking at this obscure place in relation to a king hundreds of years before Nostradamus's lifetime?[2]

The popular belief is that there is some connection between the ancient Mongols and the Book of Revelations insofar as Nostradamus appears to make reference to the raising of the dead—"to resuscitate the great King of Angoulmois"[3]—i.e., that the Second Advent will bring Christ back to raise Attila the Hun from his rotting grave and judge him for his dastardly deeds, or something of that kind. This seems somewhat obscure. There may be a much simpler reason for the use of the town as a symbol.

Let's look a little further into the future of Attila the Hun. In fact, let's move right forward to the time of Nostradamus himself.

During Nostradamus's early years, around 1524 when he was eighteen, a man named Giovanni da Verrazano served the French king Francis I, from 1515 to 1547. Francis I also happened to be Count of Angouleme, being part of the French royal dynasty of Valois (the same dynasty to which Catherine de' Medici belonged).

Verrazano traveled a very long distance to a remote island off the coast of a country that had been visited some years earlier by Christopher Columbus. Verrazano called this island Angouleme after his master's title Count of Angouleme. It later became known as Manhattan Island. One of the bridges leading out of Manhattan is named after the island's founder—Verrazano Bridge.

Nostradamus would have known all about "Angouleme," and if we believe in his powers of "sight," he would have had at least some idea about what this small island was going to turn out to be some years later. This simply and effectively connects the prediction at the top of this section with New York's Manhattan Island.

The connections with the Book of Revelation are also traditionally tied together by turning the numbers 999 upside down to make 666—the sign of the "Beast of the Apocalypse"—the Devil. This may have some significance if we consider how many of the prophet's predictions have a strong flavor of religious doom, but it seems less sensible to worry too much about this.

So, we have a "terrifying" leader likely to appear from the sky around the years perhaps between 1999 and 2001 over New York City, which will devastate the city (Angoulmois/Manhattan). Sounds pretty accurate, even though the date is two years off. But in truth, all this got us nowhere in terms of saving lives. First, the date was wrong, so where do you start looking? Second, who would have figured out that Angoulmois might mean Manhattan, and third, from what part of the sky might the devastation occur? One of the few (there is only truly one other verse that quotes an actual date among the 1,000 verses in the *Centuries*) quatrains that contains an actual date, therefore, gave very little other evidence of the event itself, even though it is a very famous verse among those who study the Prophet. Most of the effective verses are linked to other verses and have much more information, so that one of the most devastating events in the history of humankind was not mapped in sufficient detail to make any positive impact on our sensibilities of our future before September 2001. More's the pity.

Nevertheless, Nostradamus's work has given us a great deal, and the more we concentrate on the original material, the more chance we have of making something of it. And the rest of this book is about just that concentration—perhaps some of it to good effect.

THE PROPHECIES—
OLD AND YOUNG

2003 GLOBAL ECONOMIES

The inflated imitations of gold and silver which
after the rapture are thrown into the fire,
all is exhausted and dissipated by the debt. All
scrips and bonds are wiped out.
At the fourth pillar dedicated to Saturn, split by
earthquake and flood: Vexing everyone
an urn of gold is found and then restored.
—C8 V28/29[1]

Here, Nostradamus describes modern currency at the beginning of the twenty-first century, and the highly inflated "rapture" of stock market and currency activity that gathered speed throughout 1998 and 1999. He tells us that debt dissipates energy, and eventually many financial instruments are wiped out.

In the verses of this series, the prophet refers to the father figure of the world's financial activity, America (Saturn), which at this time is (incidentally) "split" by earthquakes and floods, much like what occurred during the latter part of 1998, but discovers an "urn of gold" that restores the situation back to normal. He continues by telling us that this new "treasure"

causes all manner of problems in itself—"vexing everyone"—
before solving the problem. The process of the unfolding
changes in our global currencies is likely to be quite long, and
at the end of the old millennium and the beginning of the new
may not have seemed at all obvious, given the highly buoyant
market. However, it is worth considering some of the following information in light of Nostradamus's hints.

Personal financial value is actually determined by an
extraordinary global movement that is not at all obvious, even
to stock traders. Some two trillion U.S. dollars are traded *each
day* in foreign exchange markets, one hundred times more
than the trading volume of all the world's stock markets put
together. A mere 2 percent of these foreign exchange transactions are concerned with the movements of real goods and
services in the world, while 98 percent are purely speculative
(i.e., concerned with "futures" and the expectations of currency fluctuations that have not yet taken place).[2] In effect,
these transactions are based on fantasy, the "inflated imitations of gold and silver" Nostradamus alludes to at the beginning of this series of verses. This fantasy of unreal global activity is likely to cause a massive foreign exchange crisis not
unlike the one that shook Mexico from 1994 to 1995 and Asia
from 1997 to 1998, but on a far larger scale. This would bring
about a global money meltdown, and then global depression.

Money is no longer a local matter, restricted within a
country; it is connected to every other country's money. This
means that when U.S. dollars run into problems after "the rapture" at the beginning of the twenty-first century, the entire
world will suffer the repercussions. Gone are the days of
purely national economic depressions. In fact, the old national

characteristics of financial wealth are giving way to corporate wealth. Of the hundred richest world economies, 51 percent are now corporations. General Motors, for example, is bigger financially than Denmark, and the Ford Corporation is bigger financially than South Africa. The sales of the world's two hundred largest corporations, which amounts to a staggering seven trillion U.S. dollars, are larger than the combined gross domestic product of 182 countries (all but the nine largest nations). Power—including the power to create money—is shifting away from the nation-states, which means that companies will become the dominant governing structures in the twenty-first century. In fact, in some cases, such as with Microsoft, this is already the case. With the collapse of ENRON we can see just what the impact of corporate implosion is capable of. How many other giant companies are in the same state but not admitting it?[3]

The age of the Internet, one of the most important components of the Information Age, has already given birth to its own "netmarket cash" for Internet commerce. Frequent-flyer miles are evolving toward a private currency for the traveling elite. This is part of the "urn of gold" Nostradamus refers to in the last line of the last verse of his remarkable prophecy. Sixteen hundred local communities in the world, including more than a hundred in the United States, are now issuing currency independent of the national money system.[4] Some communities, like in Ithaca, New York, issue paper currency; others in Canada, Australia, the United Kingdom, and France issue local electronic money.[5] All of this is part of an irreversible process of change in our money system and our societies. We are in a transition period, an interval of great risk but also great opportunity.

What could this "urn of gold" be that is found to be so restorative after "all scrips and bonds are wiped out"? Could it be fresh life breathed into the terrible rigors and deprivations of the economic systems of the world during the twentieth century? The very basis of modern economics for the average earner anywhere in the world is founded on greed and scarcity, an unhappy state for most of us. To illustrate the current situation, we might consider the following statistic— there are 471 billionaires in the world today. The combined worth of this tiny fraction of the world's money-making population is more than half of the wealth of the rest of the world! Perhaps in the twenty-first century some greater equality will result.

In Bernard Lietaer's *The Future of Money*, the Belgian economist gives one important suggestion as to how this might change in the future. If all the "imitations of gold and silver" are "thrown into the fire" after "the rapture," what could take their place? Lietaer suggests a greater preponderance of local currencies. These currencies would not operate as the only form of money available. We would all continue to earn the almighty dollar on a global currency basis, but there would also be the opportunity for more creative work in the local community, this work being perhaps more satisfying. There would be no interest payable on borrowing or lending, and the currency chosen would simply act as an exchange system for actual work done, unlike national currencies, which are what we might call "invisible earners" for organizations such as banks and investment organizations, which function purely on speculative activities, without providing any service to the community.[6]

If your family lived in the 1930s in Western Europe, the United States, Canada, or Northern Mexico—the areas where the Great Depression hit hardest—you may have heard about a path that could have been taken at that time. In the aftermath of Germany's hyperinflation period of the 1920s, or of the stock market crash of 1929 in other countries, literally thousands of communities started their own currency systems. Your village or town probably had one.[7]

In Germany, the Reich mark completely collapsed in the 1920s. In other countries, the national currency had become unbearably scarce because of bank and business failures in the 1930s. People who had any money tended to hoard it out of fear of the future, which in turn made it worse for everyone else.[8]

The overriding objective of the complementary currency systems of the 1930s was to ensure that people had the medium of exchange necessary for their activities by giving them work. In the more sophisticated implementations, an incentive was built to avoid currency hoarding.

The unemployed don't earn money. If enough of your clients are unemployed, businesses also fail, further increasing the number of unemployed, which brings down even bigger businesses, and so on. This effect was snowballing throughout the Western world after the initial shock of the crash of the 1920s had been absorbed. Money is really only an agreement within a community to use something as a means of exchange. So these people agreed to accept pieces of paper issued locally, metal tokens, or whatever else they could settle on. All manner of items were used—rabbit tails in Olney, Texas, by the local Chamber of Commerce, a currency that also had the desired side effect of reducing an excess of jackrabbits in the area; seashells inscribed with the seal of the Harter Drug Company in Pismo Beach, California; and wooden discs engraved with the words "In God We Trust," manufactured by the Cochrane Lumber Company in Petaluma, California.

Once the currency was created, the next problem was ensuring that people did not hoard it. Every time someone hoards currency, its lack of circulation prevents other people in the community from being able to perform transactions. The more sophisticated forms of complementary currency of the 1930s included a circulation incentive recommended by Argentinean-German businessman and economist Silvio Gesell. The idea was to encourage people to circulate money through an antihoarding tax called "demurrage." The back of each note had twelve places (one for each month of the year) where a stamp could be fixed. Any note, in order to remain valid, had to have its stamps up-to-date. These stamps could be purchased with complementary currency at shops participating in the scheme, and each stamp cost one-twelfth the value of the bill. After one year, therefore, the users would have paid the value of the bill in demurrage taxes, and the bill would then be thrown away. This is what we could call a self-liquidating currency. Many U.S. Depression currencies had this same stamp feature.

The German Wara System

By 1923, the German official currency had become totally useless. To give an idea of how this happened, we can look at the exchange rate of the Weimar currency against the U.S. dollar.

Before World War I (1913), the value of one U.S. dollar was 4.2 marks; by the end of the war, it had risen to 8 marks. In 1921, it was worth 184, and a year later 7,350. In the summer of 1923, a U.S. Congressman, A.P. Andrew, reported that he had received 4 billion marks in exchange for seven dollars, and had paid 1.5 billion marks for a restaurant meal, leaving a 400-million-mark tip!

The game stopped when, on November 18, 1923, one dollar bought 4.2 *trillion* marks. By then, 92,844,720 trillion marks were in circulation. Postage stamps cost billions, paying for a loaf of bread required a wheelbarrow full of money. Daily wage negotiations preceded work, and salaries were paid twice per day and spent within the hour.

The hero of this story is a Dr. Hebecker, the owner of a coal mine in the small town of Schwanenkirchen. He managed to secure a loan in a special temporary currency at that time, called the Rentenmark, which he hoped would save his business for a few more weeks. He gathered all of his workers and explained that they had a simple choice—either he paid them with the money from the loan and the mine would close within a month, or they could be paid in the coal they were mining. After a lot of shouting and arguing, they went as a group to see the baker and the butcher and explained that they needed to accept payment for bread and sausages in coal. The butcher and the baker, in turn, went to see their suppliers, and so on . . .

In this way the "Wara" currency was born, *wara* being a compound name in German meaning "commodity money." The Wara currency consisted of a piece of paper fully backed by coal, and to cover storage costs it also had a small monthly stamp fee. This fee, a form of demurrage tax, ensured that the money would circulate within the community.

The Wara currency saved not only Dr. Hebecker's coal mine and the whole town of Schwanenkirchen, it started circulating in wider and wider areas. It became a centerpiece of the Freiwirtschaft ("Free Economy") movement, whose foundations came from Silvio Gesell's work. More than two thousand corporations throughout Germany began using this alternative currency. Although this currency could not be inflationary because its value was tied to the value of coal, it was considered much too successful by the central bank, so the government made the Wara illegal.

The next thing to happen was a return to the unemployment line. It had become impossible for people to help themselves on a local level, leaving only one option: a strong centralized solution. The answer was found in the Bierhallen of Bavaria, where an obscure Austrian immigrant began to attract increasingly excited audiences each time he delivered his fiery speeches. His name was Adolf Hitler.

Although no one is suggesting, even Nostradamus, that the situation will be as dramatic during this millennium as it was in the late 1930s and mid-1940s, the consequences of a collapse of the U.S. currency systems would perhaps, as the prophet suggests, bring about an opportunity to change the stresses and inequalities of money usage for the better. Better money, better community, and even better individual psychology in the world of the next century.

2003 SUSTAINING AN ABUNDANT FUTURE

. . . the new generation kills hunger and fear will depart.

—C1 V69[1]

One of the best definitions of sustainability in relation to human behavior is to leave a place in better shape than we found it. Another, more formal definition is the one used by the Gro Brundlandt Report for the United Nations in 1987—sustainability is characteristic of a society that "satisfies its needs without diminishing the prospects of future generations."[2] We might add to this that it should also respect the needs and diversity of other life-forms.

Abundance does not refer to a mechanical accumulation of things; rather, abundance is what provides the freedom of choice to as many people as possible in the material domain, so we can all express our inner and outer needs and our creativity. Such creativity is the expression of our highest form of consciousness, and our highest calling, providing *meaning* in our lives. People who are starving and whose children are dying from starvation will not be able to express creativity in any way.

We may have the opportunity, according to Nostradamus's predictions, to experience sustainable abundance in this new millennium. This will be capitalism with a human face. More than a dozen countries have already successfully implemented complementary currency systems that reduce unemployment, and heal or rebuild community.[3]

It may even be possible to create a new global currency in partnership with the existing national currencies, which could deal with the conflicts between short-term financial interests and the long-term ecological sustainability. There are currently no applications of this kind of currency.

According to Lietaer's *The Future of Money*, financial changes in the world at the beginning of this new millennium are already converging to give "sustainable abundance" a chance.[4]

The core thesis of sustainable abundance is simple enough to understand: it is possible through initiatives in the money system to make capitalism truly sustainable, not only ecologically but also sociopolitically. In short, capitalism with a human face does not have to remain an oxymoron.

The window of opportunity has opened. Can we take advantage of the coming changes, and change the future ourselves?

Nostradamus concerns himself with financial change in this century in many of his verses throughout the *Centuries*— with various crises that occur in the modern stock market— and was quite successful at predicting patterns of change in the future, all the way from times when money literally did not exist through the new banking systems implemented by the Rothschilds and others, right up to our coming future when currencies become more diverse and problems arise from "global" or multinational currency requirements that have already begun to emerge in Europe, for example. The prophet even predicts, with some clarity, the time in the future when there will be one main global currency for all nations, with many hundreds of particular kinds of currency that will be used, not for national boundaries, but for corporate and private needs. This occurs, however, outside our purview and somewhat beyond 2025.

Later in the book we will look at specific changes in population growth, famine, extinction of animal life, and climate. These prophecies look a great deal more gloomy than the prospect of a sustainable existence on this planet. Nostradamus often does this—seeming on occasion to contradict himself in different quatrains about events that he saw occurring in the future, but one of his main themes in relation to the future was that time bends, so to speak, and even splinters into many parts. It is almost as though he saw that the future might even be made up of several, or even many different, dimensions—continuing stories that split and then split again, so that our actions in the present, and those of our past, directly influence the way the future pans out. We are the founders of the future. Our contemporary actions at any given time influence the way the future works. We might have a sustainable future, or, if our actions are different, more neglectful, this may result in a devastation of the life on this planet in the future. Consciousness is everything after all.

2003 THE THIRD ANTICHRIST

Mabus will soon die and there will come terrible defeat for people and animals: then suddenly one will see vengeance, hundreds suffer thirst and hunger.

—C2 V62[1]

One of the aspects of history, past and future, in which Nostradamus made his name is his identification of "Antichrists." An Antichrist is, in the most specific sense, someone who is against Christ. In a more poetic definition, and one that better suits the attitude of the twenty-first century, the Antichrist is essentially the epitome of evil—the devil incarnate. Nostradamus identified Napoleon as Antichrist number one, largely because he saw a character who he imagined would devastate the French monarchy; Hitler as Antichrist number two, for obvious reasons; and an individual named Mabus as number three.

Mabus is due to appear publicly, according to most interpretations of Nostradamus's expectations, during the early years of the twenty-first century, and to rise to power during the first years. He is said to appear from the Middle East and to have a tooth (or possibly two teeth) in the back of his throat. He rules through "love" and dies at the hand of an assassin quite early in his career, but nevertheless creates some serious havoc along the way. Is this Osama Bin Laden? It would be convenient to suppose so. Bin Laden, however, if we take Nostradamus to be our guide, does not (as far as we know) have any teeth in the back of his throat and certainly does not take his position as one associated with love, except perhaps among his own people—which according to Nostradamus is an essential aspect of his career.

Almost every decade of the last half of the twentieth century included candidates for this unpleasant character—Colonel Khaddafi in Libya, the Ayatollah Khomeini in Iran, Saddam Hussein in Iraq, and in the last year of the century, Slobadan Milosevic in Yugoslavia. What is most extraordinary is not the horrendous behavior of such individuals, though this in itself is about as disgusting as humanity can demonstrate, but the fact that the rest of us continue to allow a single human being to cause such destruction and such discomfort to the world. Leaders appear from nowhere, and it is not until the situation is far beyond our control that these individuals demonstrate they are nothing much more than absurd criminals, in Milosevic's case with a record as long as your arm. Yet they are permitted to control millions of lives.

What this says about Antichrists is that we want them. We delude ourselves into believing them to be essential to their local environments, politically, and by the time they have reached the top of the tree it is too late to knock them down.

The name Mabus, given to the expected third Antichrist by

Nostradamus, may be related to a character who lived at the same time as the prophet not far from his home. Maubus was a well-known Dutch painter who settled in France and made a name for his work. The name *Maubus*, which the painter took from the village he lived in, means "bad place."

Given all the complexities and name games Nostradamus used for his prophecies, this interpretation seems fairly typical—that the third Antichrist is not a person but a time and a place that are bad—maybe *our* time and place. The idea of the third Antichrist not being a single individual, as the other two proved to be, fits well with many other predictions that the prophet made about our particular era—the era of the twentieth century, which as seen from the sixteenth century must clearly have appeared a time of permanent and tragic war, from World War I through World War II, Korea, Vietnam, the wars in Israel and Palestine, the Yugoslav struggles, Afghanistan, etc., etc., etc.—nonstop conflict through virtually the whole century, and into this century, which we dearly hope will not be the same.

There have been so many single individuals who fit the title "Antichrist" that it seems we might want to stop looking for scapegoats for our absurd behavior and start to see that we, each and every one of us, are responsible for what is happening. At the drop of a hat, we go to war, occupying our news broadcasts, our movies, our TV programs with endless battles among any number of adversaries. In short, we relish war, as though it were an outlet for the aggressive and pugnacious spirit that resides in our hearts and minds, but there is always the "bad guy," the "Antichrist," who stands above the rest to

take the blame. The concept that Nostradamus imbues within
the interpretation above shows us the possibility that the third
Antichrist is not a person but our time and our place—an
essentially bad place that needs urgent repair. Further discus-
sion of the Antichrist concept follows later.

2003 EXTINCTION, OVERPOPULATION, FAMINE, AND CLIMATE

The great famine that I sense coming, often chang-
ing, and then becoming global, will be so great and
long that people will take roots from the ground, and
children from the breast.

—C1 V67[1]

This is the first of a series of verses that deal with world population. Later in the book the reader will find further details of
how this will affect us in more specific areas of life. This section is devoted to population, climate, and famine. A later section deals with rural and city effects.

An extraordinary shift in the rate of population growth
occurred around two centuries ago with man's harnessing of
fossil fuels. Until the nineteenth century, nature was seen as
an awe-inspiring force over which humans had little or no
impact. Over the past 150 million years, new species had been
created at a rate exceeding the rate of extinction. In the past
two centuries alone all that has changed. By 1800 the number
of animal extinctions exceeded the number of new species for

the first time. Over the past few decades this process has accelerated to the extent that the collision course between the "needs" of humans and the well-being of the rest of the biosphere has reached unprecedented proportions. In 1996, the World Conservation Union, in collaboration with more than six hundred scientists, published the most comprehensive survey on the status of animal life on earth. Their conclusion was as follows: 25 percent of mammal and amphibian species, 11 percent of birds, 20 percent of reptiles, and 34 percent of fish species surveyed are threatened with extinction. Another 5–14 percent of species are "nearing threatened status."[2] This is the biggest mass extinction process since the dinosaurs sixty-five million years ago, but unlike the dinosaurs we are not just contemporaries of a mass destruction—we are the cause of it.

These were the facts in 1999:

Human population: 5.978 billion

Projected population by 2025: 7.824 billion

Increase in human population per day: 194,000 (this is a small reduction from the previous two-year projection)

Years until insufficient land—northern food supply: 6

Years until insufficient land—southern food supply: 37

Species extinctions per day: 104

Years until one-third of remaining species are lost: 7

State of the World Indicators[3]

Biosphere II, a Colorado project whose objective was to sustain humans and animals in a completely controlled environment, cost $200 million and many years of planning and preparation. After seventeen months, the project was abandoned because of uncontrollable air and water pollution. Nineteen of the twenty-five animal species went extinct. The one species that thrived were cockroaches.[4]

We may see all of this as irrelevant to our personal lives today, but soon it will be quite relevant indeed. If human population increases at the rate indicated in the above chart between the years 2000 and 2050—and also given the fact that population *growth rate* is speeding up—there will be three times as many people on this planet by 2050 or earlier. That's three times as many people walking the streets of New York City (if it exists); three times as many people trying to get aboard Tokyo subways (impossible); three times as many people living outside the city centers and within the suburban towns; three times as many people lining up for hospital treatment, schooling, university education, supermarket checkouts, in rush-hour traffic, and vacationing on our beaches; and three times as many people eating the food that is supplied by the land, the oceans, and the animals.

At the same rate of animal extinction, by 2050 there will be only humans on this planet—no birds, no animals, no insects, no fish—only us. In effect we will have accomplished exactly what we fear in our worst science fiction fantasies—"Independence Day" will have arrived. We will have taken over the earth and wiped out all other natural occupants. We *are* the aliens, with only poverty and famine to show for our efforts.

In this and in other series of verses, Nostradamus tells this story, filling in the details of how it unfolds, when it occurs (astrologically), and even what the climate conditions will be at that time. We will examine the following prophecy in more detail later in this book, in a place where it serves an additional purpose. Here we use it to illustrate the expected climate changes:

> *The scythe joined with the pond towards*
> *Sagittarius, at the high point of its ascendant,*
> *sickness, famine and death will occur through war,*
> *and the century is approaching its renewal. For*
> *forty years the rainbow will not appear, for forty*
> *more it will be seen each day: the parched earth will*
> *again become dry, and then great floods will return*
> *again.*
>
> *—C1 V16/17[5]*

At a time when "the scythe joins with the pond toward Sagittarius, at the high point of its ascendant" (Saturn in Aquarius at the height of Sagittarius's ascendant—between 1999 and 2003, and then again in 2015), we're told by the prophet that climate changes will take place rapidly, from drought to flood and back to drought in the space of months ("the rainbow will not appear . . ."). It's good to remember that Nostradamus was something of a poet, and often expressed what he saw in terms that were never intended to be entirely accurate but rather to point toward tendencies. If we take a look at climate trends today, we find, remarkably, that modern scientists agree with his predictions.

In the past century, engineers whose job it was to design

storm sewers, bridges, and culverts would plan for "hundred-year storms," assuming it was sufficient to strengthen the basic drainage systems to last for the eventuality of only one major storm, or a series of storms equivalent to one major storm, per century. Thomas Karl of the National Oceanic and Atmospheric Administration, says, "There isn't really a hundred-year event anymore. We seem to be getting these storms of the century every couple of years."[6]

Some storms of 1997 and 1998 have already qualified for the title "five-hundred-year storms." Charles Keeling of the Scripps Institution of Oceanography has shown that spring starts about a week earlier than previous decades globally and that temperature swings are broadening.[7] Furthermore, there is more evidence that permanent climate change is possible in the remarkably short time lapse of decades instead of centuries, as was thought up until now.

The freezing level of the atmosphere—the height at which the air temperature reaches freezing—has been gaining altitude at the rate of nearly fifteen feet a year since 1970. Tropical glaciers are melting at what the Ohio State University researchers term "striking rates."[8] Ellen Mosley Thompson of the University Team says, "The Lewis glacier on Mount Kenya has lost 40 percent of its mass, in the Ruwenzori all the glaciers are in massive retreat. Everything in Patagonia is retreating. We've seen that plants are moving up the mountain. I frankly don't know what additional evidence you need."[9]

The European research satellites ERS-1 and ERS-2 have shown that the West Atlantic ice sheet in Antarctica is receding at the rate of more than one kilometer (three-fifths of a mile) per year. Barclay Kamb, a noted glaciologist at Caltech, comments, "I was rather skeptical of this idea of Antarctic ice sheet disintegration. . . . But now, the evidence for rapid ice changes is good enough that the worst-case scenarios are worth worrying about. . . . If the ice sheet disintegrated, sea levels would rise by about five meters (twenty feet)."[10] This would drown many coastlines around the world, transform most harbor cities into swamps, and make many islands in the Pacific uninhabitable.

Sixteen hundred scientists, including a majority of living Nobel Prize winners in the sciences, have unanimously agreed on the following public warning: "A great change in stewardship of the earth and the life on it is required, if vast human misery is to be avoided and our global home on this planet is not to be *irretrievably mutilated.*"[11]

In a separate initiative, a global meeting of economists came to a similar conclusion in 1997.[12]

2004 THE UNITED STATES OF AMERICA

Surrounded by three seas, a great nation will be born with its most important holiday on a Thursday [Thanksgiving]. The fame, praise, rule and power of this place will grow greater and greater, by land and sea, with great power also to the East.

—C1 V50[1]

The earth and air will freeze a great water, when they come to venerate Thursday: that which will result, never was so fair before, from the four parts they will come to honor it.

—C10 V71[2]

The first of these two verses is an almost perfect description of the United States of America. The United States is surrounded by three seas, has a unique holiday on a Thursday each year at Thanksgiving, and certainly continues to fulfill the last sentence. There is no downside to this prophecy, as there very often is with other verses. Almost invariably, when

Nostradamus defines a place or a person of great growth and success, a last line indicates the inevitability of collapse or a dreadful fate of some kind. Here, all we get is that this place will grow "greater and greater." Given the many other verses that describe circumstances under which the United States will largely flourish, perhaps we may truly look forward to this massive collection of states becoming even more powerful in the twenty-first century. No other empire in the past has lasted forever—Ancient Egypt, Greece, Rome, Austria, England—they all fell apart sooner or later. Perhaps Nostradamus is telling us here that America may go long on the course.

The second verse is more enigmatic, and pinpoints a few specific events, making reference once again to the land that has the "Thursday" holiday—this is uniquely America. The first line indicates a new Ice Age, something that scientists have predicted for some time. But according to this prophecy, the result will not be as terrible as we might expect. The rest of the verse creates a sense that America will become (perhaps already has become) a country to be highly venerated throughout the world.

To look more closely at this we have included on these pages the natal chart of the United States, based on the time of the signing of the Declaration of Independence. Examining the characteristics created by the planetary positions at the time of America's birth, we discover a picture in which we can believe with some degree of confidence. One of the most significant aspects within the chart is the Mercury and Pluto opposition. This configuration within any chart signifies an interest in the hidden side of life, and a great subtlety of vision. This might give rise to the preponderance of spirituality and religion. This characteristic also produces an ability to penetrate to the core of a situation and recognize its truth in others.

Negatively, the U.S. chart signifies an obsession with secrecy, deception, and undercover dealings. Such a chart in a human individual would tend to produce a very effective liar. As a national characteristic it has its good points, such as a willingness to absorb psychic phenomenon and to pay attention to the complexities and subtleties of psychology and the esoteric. University courses in the United States cover so many fields of the esoteric that for those looking for a university qualification in these areas, it's hard to make a choice! In the United Kingdom, for example, there isn't even a complete course on C.G. Jung, one of the world's greatest psychologists and philosophers and the man who gave birth to the concept of universal consciousness, except as a small part of some courses in religion.

Another negative aspect arising out of this Mercury/Pluto opposition is a tendency toward corruption and secrecy in economic dealings. The amassing of wealth might appear as an immoral or unethical preoccupation. This would not seem like a feature of America or its people, however; when we get closer to the way things are done in the United States there is a subtle morality surrounding money that might not at first appear obvious. This is supported by a general characteristic by a Mercury/Pluto opposition from Cancer to Capricorn in the U.S. natal chart, which forms a specific configuration that reflects a collective struggle in expressing thoughts and feelings, and communication that appears to be open but actually conceals a great deal beneath the surface. The ubiquitous use of jargon and politically correct words and phrases tells much of the way this works as an evasive method of interrelation. This general trend in the United States tells of the fact that things are never quite what they seem to be. By watching American TV, you will (or should be able to) notice an excessive amount of what might be described as "obvious" material—blasting noise, terrible programming, and the crude use of violence. The advertising is probably of the poorest quality in the world for its obvious characteristics. It is as though all this is a camouflage for the truth, for beneath the surface of American culture there is more brewing than one might ever imagine, and the "cover-up" hides this truth effectively.

This also reflects the way in which America deals with other countries, and the way in which the government expresses itself to the people. We all watched, during 1998 and early 1999, how Congress and the House of Representatives dealt with the Clinton scandal. So much on the surface— determination, moral turpitude, and a kind of disciplinarian attitude—would have been (in fact was) considered utterly absurd in almost any European country. Who would wish to make such a massive fuss about such an unimportant feature of a president who in all other aspects was one of the best to appear in U.S. history? But beneath the surface of all this noise and opinion, the deep dark secrets of sexual repression and moral indignation, along with religious fundamentalism, fired the political drama to its greatest heights since Nixon. Here is a perfect Mercury/Pluto opposition.

Looking forward, therefore, using Nostradamus's indications and the astrological characteristics of the United States as a nation, we find fascinating changes afoot. Between 2000 and 2012, America will see a period of great calm and success. A number of interesting transits in the chart give us indications. Uranus reaches the conjunction with America's natal moon in Aquarius, heralding a greater role for women in the national psyche. Transiting Uranus forms this conjunction throughout 2002 and the first half of 2003. It is not a global or malevolent aspect but reflects a period of great change in terms of the role of women. According to this indication, we can possibly expect a woman presidential candidate, or even a woman president, in the year 2004.

Another, less attractive scenario results from these same transits: a rise of religious fundamentalism that would in turn reflect a kind of collective emotional breakdown. Between 2014 and 2016, the astrological readings correspond with the ascendance of Sagittarius, meaning Saturn will cross the country's ascendant. It will be a time of great soul searching, of facing harsh realities. In an individual chart such a time would probably coincide with a considerable change in fortune— even a redefinition of a life pattern. For a nation, this might not be terrible, but it will certainly be sobering.

Saturn will also transit in opposition to America's natal Uranus in Gemini, suggesting a reevaluation of what Americans have considered freedom. This might relate to prejudice.

Another significant transit during this time is that of Pluto with Capricorn, bringing it into opposition with America's Venus, Jupiter, and the sun, all of which will be lined up in Cancer. In the birth chart, this group of planets is in the seventh house. Nationally speaking, this is the house of allies and enemies. This transit reflects a complete shift in America's relationships with other countries, economically and through involvement with the United Nations or NATO. It reflects conflict and competition on economic and political levels. Most important, it tells us about a change in the definition of government. The transit of Pluto to the natal sun was the aspect in force during the collapse of the Soviet Union (to illustrate the potential scale of such an astrological change), and this will take place during the first years of the new century and millennium.

At the same time, Uranus in Aries is in square to America's sun in Cancer, so it is certainly a radical transformation. These aspects involve relationships with other countries.

There is no indication in all this of any holocaust or Armageddon. Nothing in the astrology of the United States or, indeed, in Nostradamus's prophecies gives the clear picture that somehow Christ will rise again and the end of the world will be nigh. These seem, in the light of a more sensible application of a poetic, prophetic mind, more likely expressions of drama and change. During the latter part of the twentieth century, in fact, we saw major events that might have given rise to the idea of an end-of-the-world scenario, but in reality earth and humankind recover—so far. Changes will be exciting, however, if a bit more down-to-earth in nature.

2005 THE SCIENCE OF SPACE AND TIME

Space brings many opportunities for creative choice,
as human ingenuity brings man closer to the uni-
verse. Understanding of death makes man greater,
earlier than we might expect, the answers appear.
— C2 V45[1]

When Sir Isaac Newton revealed his understanding of the laws of gravity in the seventeenth century, the scientific community of the time, and for many years after, believed they had discovered the way the universe worked. Creation was like an enormous clockwork machine, and God was the watchmaker. The religions of the time dismissed the idea, of course, but then religion has long confused the issue of reality with all manner of absurdities. By the end of the nineteenth century and into the early years of the twentieth century, cracks appeared in Newton's laws with the arrival of quantum theory, which explained the fact that the atomic world—that which exists beneath the structure of matter as an apparently solid substance—did not conform with the tidy laws of nature as observed by science. A spanner was thrown into the works, which told us that if the microcosm of life—the atomic building blocks of what we perceive to be true with our senses—does not behave in the same way as the macrocosm—that which is built upon the atom—how can that which we perceive be true? The atomic microcosm of our world proved to be chaotic and unpredictable, so how come the macrocosm didn't behave in the same way?

At this same time, or just before, Albert Einstein's theories of special relativity smashed another spanner into the clockwork-universe theory by inferring, and then proving, that space and time could be warped by the movement and speed of the observer. If you traveled into space at a speed close to that of light, when you returned the planet would have aged much more rapidly than you had. If a spaceship were to fall into a black hole, then it would appear to stretch longer and longer before disappearing. How could this be? And why wasn't God's creative law as clear and sensible as it had appeared to be thousands of years before?

And in any event, the two theories—relativity and quantum physics—were also incompatible. So neither God nor modern science actually had the answers. Could God be throwing dice just to confuse us or, more likely, did science not know all the answers after all—yet?

Nostradamus implies in a number of verses, including the one above, that our movement into space travel and the science this requires us to develop—combined with our growing understanding of how our lives and our processes of life and death work—bring us closer to understanding the very foundation of science. He adds that the final answers arrive "earlier than we might expect."

This fundamental understanding may already be upon us,

an understanding that will certainly develop rapidly in the first decade of this new millennium. It's called "string theory."[2]

String theory, or superstring theory, is now seen as the "Theory of Everything," rather like all of the previous theories from Newton to quantum mechanics, but with what appears to be a remarkable difference. String theory brings together the macro and the micro, tying the universe (and with a very exciting string) into a package that might well be the concept physics has been seeking for many years. Matter, all the way from a piece of wood right up to a whole planet, is made up of molecules and atoms. Within each atom are electrons that spin about a nucleus in the same way the moon spins about the earth. Within each nucleus, in turn, are protons and neutrons, which then subdivide still further into quarks. Until recently these "invisible" building blocks were believed to be the very smallest aspects of life's matter. String theory goes a stage further—or smaller. Strings are tiny bundles of energy that vibrate in patterns that correspond to whatever structure they occupy. If these strings are the basis of all matter, then the universe is a sort of vibrating "instrument," perhaps functioning on dimensional planes we have no experience of at all. Solid things are suddenly not at all solid. These minute strings of vibrating energy are not in any way fixed, material, or solid.

But we experience mass and matter as being hard and dependable. How can a table, for example, be made up of a shimmering string of energy? Perhaps, say physicists, a table is observed that way, sensed that way, only because such is human conditioning. We might go completely crazy if we saw how matter truly exists, so we filter out every sense and experience that does not correspond to our conditioned beliefs.

Our brains have organized life in a way we can accept, whereas the reality is something quite different. When we see a chair made of wood, all that is really happening is the arrival of reflected light from the chair, which the brain then interprets as such. A chair is only a chair because we have learned to give it that label. Does seeing a chair truly mean we are seeing a wooden item of a certain shape, or are we simply experiencing what the brain has led us to believe is a chair? String theory suggests that we may be living in more than three dimensions—try eleven! Brian Greene, who discusses string theory in *The Elegant Universe*, uses the example of an ant on a garden hose. Viewed from a distance, one could say that the ant can move in only two dimensions, one way or the other along the hose. If we get closer, however, we see that the ant could also move around the cylindrical dimension of the hose. Greene suggests that within the universe there may be other dimensions, like the girth of the hose, so small we cannot perceive them yet.[3]

Nostradamus tells us not only of space "out there" but of space itself as a dimension of our lives, and he does this from more than four centuries ago, when science was still fighting with the Roman Catholic Church over whether the earth was flat or round.

2005 THE NEW WORLD ORDER:
THE FUTURE OF CHINA

*One day the great powers will become friends, and
their power will increase. America will be at the
height of its power. To the man of blood the opportunity will be given.*

—*C2 V89[1]*

*The two will not remain united for long, and in thir-
teen years they will surrender to the Middle East.
There will be much loss on both sides, and Pope
Peter will be needed.*

—*C5 V78[2]*

*In a place and time when flesh will not readily
weaken, the common law will change: the old will
gain strength, and longer life. Communism is left
far behind.*

—*C4 V32[3]*

The first two verses above indicate a friendship or joint accord between the United States and another great power. Many interpreters have attributed the verses to the United States and the former Soviet Union. Events in the last few years of the twentieth century have rather put this interpretation aside, as the Baltic States, even Russia, can hardly be described as great any more. Also, America is still reaching "the height of its power," and any accord between the United States and Russia has not resulted in an increase in their joint power. What we are actually seeing, at the time of writing in 2001, is the likelihood of Russia falling through levels of poverty and political weakness at a frightening rate. Given astrological readings that we will examine in this chapter, China seems a better candidate for any future partnership.

The significant aspect of the first two verses is the timing of America's power peak, as it is referred to many times in Nostradamus's verses, often related to financial wealth and the "rapture," mentioned previously, of the stock market, followed by a collapse of currencies and market buoyancy.

We cannot, of course, be sure of the time when the United States will reach the height of its power, for the moment this happens is presumably the same moment in which the power begins to turn on a downward path. The stock market's Dow Jones Industrial Average broke the ten thousand mark some time ago, the highest peak ever. But when will it break the eleven thousand or the twelve thousand or even the twenty thousand mark? Not even Nostradamus gave us such precise pointers. But other observations may help us pinpoint likely dates when two great powers will join hands for their mutual advantage. And according to the second verse above, thirteen years after this accord the two powers will part company again because of Middle Eastern crises or changes in power. Astrologically, the date of the accord appears to be 2005, making the breakup in 2016.

The "man of blood" is either the U.S. president—perhaps the president elected in the year 2004—or his or her equivalent in China, both of whom will have the opportunity to make this powerful accord. Other verses back this up, as the reference to a man of blood is common in Nostradamus's poetic method of characterizing a particularly important individual.

We have watched China change over the past years, its population becoming one of the two largest in the world, and its politics and interests in human rights unpopular with the balance of the world's nations. It is the last truly Communist country, and as such remains a lonely entity, though friendly approaches began with President Clinton during the late twentieth century. This relationship evidently grows in the early years of the new millennium, at the hands of a "man of blood." Sadly, Nostradamus did not indicate an individual who "proclaims evil" as the significant one, but perhaps we can make a guess as to who this might be!

Astrological China

The Proclamation of the People's Republic of China occurred at noon on October 1, 1949.[4] The natal chart that results from this "birth" date has a sun/Neptune conjunction in Libra, which reflects the same kind of utopian concept we see in Germany. And while Germany's natal chart has the same conjunction as China's, the chart for China also contains a

Mars/Pluto conjunction in Leo, which provides a ruthless characteristic. Between 2011 and 2012, Pluto transits to find a square to China's natal sun when it transits through Capricorn. The resulting events indicate tremendous turmoil within the Chinese government. But if we look closely at the years prior to this crescendo of problems, we can see the way the difficulties begin and develop.

Between 2001 and 2003, Pluto crosses Communist China's ascendant in Sagittarius, reflecting the political and religious idealism so close to the ways of China's Communist founders—a kind of fanaticism similar to the fanaticism inherent in American Christian fundamentalism. This basic astrological event gives us a picture of a China beginning to experience turmoil during the first years of the twenty-first century, though the signs are that this will not be entirely visible to the rest of the world, particularly given this country's ability to hide its internal activities. But in 2011, when Pluto goes square with the natal sun, matters will reach a far greater level of seriousness.

The third verse at the top of this chapter gives us the Nostradamus clues. The prophet links new scientific changes in the power to slow down the aging process with the end of Communism: "In a place and time when flesh will not readily weaken, the common law will change: the old will gain strength, and longer life. Communism is left far behind."

2005 THE NEW WORLD OLDER AND OLDER AND OLDER

In a place and time when flesh will not readily weaken, the common law will change: the old will gain strength, and longer life. Communism is left far behind.

—C4 V32[1]

At the beginning of the third millennium, at a time when war has been so common, there will be a chance for death to end.

—C10 V74[2]

One of the most important changes in this new century is the increased presence of the older population in the Western world. More and more medicines and treatments are being developed to slow down the aging process, and Nostradamus pinpoints the timing for this as coinciding with the end of Communism, which, in the sequence of verses occurring before and after the verse above, indicate the year 2001 as being a time when China's political environment started to change most radically.

Already many new methods of body-parts replacement are being experimented with; for example, it is now possible to grow a bone-like substance.[3] Until the end of the twentieth century, treatments requiring bone transplant had to be managed with the patient's existing bone, which was usually taken from the pelvis—a painful and long process. John Davies, a dentist and biomedical engineer at the University of Toronto, and his colleagues have developed a method of growing a polymer substance very like the structure of the bone that exists beneath the level of the body's harder outer bone structure. This "trabecular" bone is a spongy substance with a massive number of interconnected pockets, similar to the sea sponges found in many bathrooms but much tougher. Osteoclasts and osteoblasts, which destroy (eat) and create new bone naturally, rejuvenating the bone structure constantly, reside within the millions of tiny crevices in the human trabecular bone structure.[4] When a synthetic polymer bone is transplanted into a patient's body, these cells spread into the new structure, healing injuries, rejuvenating the body, and providing fresh life to the aging.

We can expect other "homegrown" human rejuvenation methods, whether for various organs, skin, or even blood. All of these will reduce and perhaps eventually stop the aging process altogether.

Health Credit Cards

According to a number of geneticists, including Professors Richard Dawkins and Michio Kaku, in England, by about 2020 it will be possible to visit a doctor and get a genetic analysis that will result in a credit card embedded with a complete genetic map of your body. Even aging will be regarded as simply a curable disease. Heart attacks will never be fatal, and most organs will be grown to replace those that fail. The so-called health credit card will be something each individual will carry in the same way as we now carry driver's licenses, as it will contain the "stamp" of the person who carries it. These cards will be used for all medical emergencies and identity needs, including ATM machines and police identity. Instead of a handwritten signature, it will provide a signature of the entire body.

There *are* objections to this mechanical concept. What if the genetic code is not the only thing that creates human nature? What if there is a genetic memory derived from emotional expression—changing the body as it experiences crises, traumas, joys? What if proteins cause changes in the body and its growth—messages from other sources outside the body, for example? The passion today may be for the realization of an all-encompassing code, but we have yet to discover that such a thing exists.

Nostradamus's message relates to a future where "death ends," a future that we have not yet reached, but the fascination is not truly with an immortal capability within the human race, but what will happen when all those centuries stretch before us. Nostradamus says nothing about this.

2006 ROMAN CATHOLICISM, WORLD GOVERNMENT, AND THE NEW CONTINENT

A single monarch will be made for the world, who will not be long at peace, or alive: all this at a time when the fishing boat will be lost, after rule in great detriment.

—C1 V4[1]

This verse tells us two things: we can expect a world leader to emerge and, at the same time, the Vatican will be in trouble again, seemingly terminal trouble. The "fishing boat" is a common metaphor in Nostradamus's predictions for the Roman Catholic Church, as it makes a biblical reference to the disciples of Jesus. Later in this chapter we will also take a look at a prophecy surrounding the new continent of "Aquilas," which it is believed will result from the changes taking place in the Baltics and what was Eastern Europe. But first the fall of the Roman Catholic Church.

Many verses in the *Centuries* speak of problems in the Roman Catholic Church during the latter part of the twentieth century and the beginning of the twenty-first. Having converted from Judaism in his youth, becoming a Roman Catholic in order largely to avoid the attacks of the Spanish Inquisition, Nostradamus may have had something against the Roman Church. Much of what he predicted for the Church has been borne out over the past century, however; his prophecies surrounding Popes Pius XI and XII and then John XXIII proved remarkably correct. He also wrote extraordinary verses surrounding the 1980s banking scandals that resulted in the fall of the Vatican Banco Ambrosiano. We can expect some degree of accuracy, therefore, for the future expectations during the early years of the new millennium, when Nostradamus tells us of a major change in the Roman Church's fortunes.

These prophecies are also echoed by other famous individuals, such as the biblical prophet Saint Malachi, who in the twelfth century, while in Rome, fell into a trance and during a vision predicted and described the entire succession of 112 popes who would appear in the future. Part of his vision tells us that John Paul II will be followed by only two more popes before a major change, or even a collapse, of the Roman Catholic Church in Rome. Malachi describes the penultimate pope (following John Paul II) as "De Gloria Olivae," and Nostradamus gives his name as "Clement." Both Malachi and Nostradamus tell us that the final pope will be named Peter, after the very first pontiff of the Church following Jesus's death, thus completing the great cycle of two thousand years. A common tradition in Italy tells us that the body of Peter will be dragged throughout the city of Rome in disgrace, and the Vatican will be pillaged, the Church falling in ruin. This, according to calculations of the sequence of the prophecies in the *Centuries*, should occur in 2006, almost exactly two thousand years after the birth of Jesus.

All this coincides with another major event in the life of this rapidly changing time—the first attempt to create a world government. We are told in the same verse that "a single monarch will be made for the world . . ." It seems somehow unlikely, given the constant breaking down of nations into smaller nations in the latter years of the twentieth century, that humanity is going to get it together to create a world organization to rule this warring planet. This process has, however, already begun. More and more, the United States, partnered with the United Nations, is acting as a global police force to attempt to create peace in the Middle East, in Yugoslavia, and between the Palestinians and the Israelis. As discussed earlier, the U.S. dollar has become the most commonly measured global currency, and if the United States continues to flourish through the early years of the twenty-first century, perhaps a logical change will be toward a global community with one leader.

Nevertheless, more than half the nations of the world are currently in some form of conflict, the biggest single continent in such condition being Africa. Nostradamus hedges his bet on the success of a world government at this time with the words "who will not be long at peace, or alive. . . ." Nevertheless, this verse gives the impression that we begin to move toward a global organization to rule the whole planet in the early part of the new millennium.

Another verse, however, which follows in the same sequence of prophecies, brings a new continent into the arena at about the same time as the attempt toward world government: "A long time before such intrigues, there are those of the Orient moon [who] will gather a big corner of Aquilon." Nostradamus's assistant, Chavigny, the man who sorted through the prophet's scribbled notes after each night of trance, commented on this verse specifically: "[That it] has a very long and large extent, such that it could be called another world, if we include all of Germany, Poland, Lithuania, Livonia, Gothia, Sweden, Norway, Scandia, the isles of the Ocean and come to Muscovy, the two Sarmatias, up to the columns of Alexander and even the Caspian Sea, and take Scythia on this side of Mount Imaus, otherwise called Great Tartary; all this is part of Aquilon as well as other provinces that I do not mention."[2]

In current geography "all this" would be Russia, Poland, Germany, and Scandinavia. Those of the Orient moon can be presumed to be China. What we may be seeing here is a time when China has completed its industrial growth, around the decade of the new millennium, and literally absorbs Aquilon, the countries in Chavigny's list. Here would be a new continent as big as the United States, and bigger than the whole of Europe. Who might then be ruling the world?

2007 THE EARTH'S APOCALYPSE

*With Mars and Mercury and the moon joined
together, towards the south in India and Asia there
will be great droughts, and the earth will tremble
with earthquakes.*

—*C3 V3[1]*

*For many nights the earth will shake twice in the
Spring, Asia will be in two seas.*

—*C2 V52[2]*

*Volcanoes from the center of the earth will bring
trembling around New York. Two great faults will
make war for a long time and then Syracuse will
color a new river red.*

—*C1 V87[3]*

Nostradamus is more famous for his prophecies related to
earthquakes, volcanoes, floods, and other natural disasters
than he is for predicting almost any other type of event in

human history. But there have always been earthquakes. Some people—British biochemist James Lovelock in particular—regard the planet Earth as a living entity, an organism, containing checks and balances that maintain its processes rather like a human body.[4] In a sense, everything occurring on the planet is part of a synchronous whole that includes volcanic eruptions, massive tornadoes, and even earthquakes themselves, all part of the homeostasis of existence.

Mankind, even including some scientists, on the other hand, still believes that we can one day actually conquer nature, that we are somehow greater than our environment. This encourages the idea, absurd though it may be, that Earth and man are in a kind of struggle for survival, and that natural disasters are somehow a kind of conflict, or a revenge against the poor treatment man is currently heaping on his home. Certainly there is no excuse for our bad behavior, and certainly we suffer from this bad behavior each day, with the poor air quality in cities, the ill health brought about by convenience foods, etc. But the concept of a conflict between man and Earth is yet only another manifestation of our warring hearts. Why would God *or* planet care much for our stupidity? They are both far bigger than our tiny minds!

The Earth, however, continues to blow fuses, and according to the prophecies of Nostradamus and several other notable futurists, more are on the way during the early years of the twenty-first century. And there is little doubt that mankind is somewhat contributing to this situation through his lack of understanding of and synchronicity with his home planet.[5]

About once every minute more than forty acres of the

planet's tropical forests—designed to enrich the atmosphere—are cut down for man's convenience, becoming open
grazing land.[6] That amounts to about 120 square miles a day,
which every year equals the size of New York State—every
year, for decades! Within two years, because of the effect of
rain on the topsoils, the land is useless for crop planting. At
the current rate, by 2006, almost all of the tropical forest areas
will have been destroyed, and thus the air-purifying function
they were vital for will have ended.

The net result of this is the entrapment of the sun's heat in
our atmosphere. The loss of oxygen-producing trees, which
counteract carbon dioxide, leads to a preponderance of carbon dioxide in the atmosphere. No oxygen from the tree's pho-
tosynthesis process means no balance with the carbon dioxide. The sun's heat has no outlet, and so the planet gradually
heats up. Most of us will have noticed this during 2001 and
2002. Isn't it strange that everywhere seems to be warmer?
How pleasant . . . for the moment. But it isn't strange. It's
totally understandable and scientifically provable. What is
strange is our inability to comprehend what is actually going
on. We are slowly baking ourselves!

The famines and droughts Nostradamus speaks of are per-
fectly natural on the basis of our scientific input into the
world—our determination to dominate rather than synchro-
nize with nature. Climatologists already know that earth will
suffer the greatest drought of its entire history sometime during the early years of the new millennium. This is not a suppo-
sition but an established expectation. As discussed earlier,
storms are ever more frequent. Not long ago, major storms
occurred only once every few years. These were called "five-

year storms" or "ten-year storms" because of their rarity and size. But five-year storms are now occurring about every six months, and ten-year storms at least once a year!

Dr. Jeffrey Goodman's *We Are the Earthquake Generation* predicted, correctly, that the instance of earthquakes would increase exponentially starting in 1987.[7] He writes about a chain reaction of quakes—calling them superquakes—starting in India and moving across the planet from Asia through Greece and on to the coasts of Europe. Perhaps the so-called apocalypse predicted for the early years of the new millennium is less about interhuman war and conflict than it is about natural cataclysm.

Predictions, both from Nostradamus and from twentieth-century prophets, concur in their expectation of a series of earthquakes starting in India, one of which occurred in 1993. A sudden escalation of quakes is expected to cause major floods in India and then bring unexpected levels of disaster to Japan, after which it will move westward on the crust of the planet, causing volcanoes in Sicily (Mount Etna) and Italy (Vesuvius). The next quakes will be in the south of England and along the European coastlines. Finally, of course, is the "big one" expected along the San Andreas fault. Seismologists in the United States no longer talk about *whether* there will be a California earthquake of a major size, but *when* there will be such a quake.

When this quake hits, the oceans are expected to flood into the south end of the California deserts, breaking the coastline away from the mainland. All this is hard to predict exactly, but if we time it to coincide with the other cataclysmic prophecies related to biblical expectations and to Nostradamus's prophecies, it could all happen around the years 2005 and after.

This series of quakes is predicted to be followed by a second round of quakes that will hit the United States once the West Coast has largely vanished and broken up into small islands. East Africa and South America will break up as well, while New York and Florida will become flooded as enormous new islands rise from the oceans of the South Pacific. We could certainly view such catastrophic activity as a sort of Judgment Day.

The following words, which relate to the years 2000–2025, describe not only earthquake activity but other massive seismic movements, including a possible shift in the earth's axis: "There will be omens in the spring, and extraordinary changes thereafter, reversals of Nations and mighty earthquakes. . . . And during the month of October there shall be a massive movement of the Globe, and it will be such that there will be those who will think that the planet has lost its gravity, being plunged into the abyss of darkness."

The idea and the distinct possibility of a shift in the Earth's axis has been around for some time. The possibility of this is linked to the process we have already described of a change in the climate of the planet due to the destruction of the forest regions of South America and elsewhere, resulting in global warming. This, in turn, is already causing the ice of the poles to melt at an unprecedented rate. Many fear that this change in the balance of the planet's axis may result in a shift that will cause the whole planet to wobble—literally. There have been, according to Professor Charles Hapgood, examples of this in the past. In the book *Plate Tectronics: Earth's Shifting Crust* (Lucent Books, 1991, by Sean Grady), Hapgood suggests that during the last one hundred millennia, this may have occurred three times.[8]

2008 WOMEN AND POWER

*The Moon hidden in deep shadows, her brother
passes by rusty colored, the great one masked for a
long time beneath eclipses; iron will cool in the
bloody wound.*

—C1 V84[1]

*A new law will emerge in the new world of America,
at a time when Syria, Judea and Palestine are significant: the great barbarian empire of patriarchy
that men have created will decay during the time
that the feminine spirit is completing its cycle.*

—C2 V42[2]

For those of us who have taken the laborious trouble to read
all of Nostradamus's approximately one thousand verses, it
becomes evident that a rather large number of them seem to
make no sense at all. These are generally attributed to the
future—that unmapped country—in the hope that some day
an event will occur that will "fit" (almost) the mantle of the
prophet's vision. Otherwise, these enigmatic "quatrains" are

nothing more than the meandering of a madman who had his moments.

Or, the alternative this author prefers, Nostradamus was not concerned only with world-shattering events like wars, disasters, and royalty; he also paid attention, perhaps even unwittingly, to the softer, more delicate, and more sensitive areas of the future. One of these can be seen as the future of women, exemplified by the verses above, which, as usual, at first appear bizarre, but with a closer look become clearer. The shadowed moon refers to women, who were shadowed by the activities of men in their constant quest to conquer and dominate their female partners.

The women's movement began to grow significantly only during the twentieth century. Until the world wars, women generally had a poor deal. But according to Nostradamus, the rise of women in power will become far more significant yet. Women, "hidden in deep shadows" for centuries, intended only for marriage and childbearing and childrearing, are still hidden from the sun in many parts of the modern world. Men in Iraq, Iran, and other Islamic areas still cannot face their fear of the opposite sex, and hide their women behind costumes calculated to prevent their femininity from being manifest, altering their religious scriptures to provide an excuse for this archaic and prejudicial behavior. Even many African tribes are not this primitive.

And if the truth be known, even in Western society, in the United States and Europe, many women are still forced by their conditioning—their family beliefs and habits—into staying largely in the home and being dependent on their husbands. For a woman to rise through the levels of business achievement is still much tougher than for men in a world with male-dominated clubs, boards of directors, and medical and legal professions.

All this will change: "her brother passes by rusty colored." With a touch of wry humor, Nostradamus comments on how men will go rusty as their power diminishes, while women grow stronger in matters of the world's growth. The metaphor of "the great one masked for a long time beneath eclipses . . . iron will cool in the bloody wound" refers both to the aggression of a male-dominated world and the male sexual organ being cooled in the blood of female menstruation. Perhaps much of the future will change when men no longer rule the planet so aggressively, and women get a chance to find us all a more peaceful coexistence. How different it might be if Iraq were ruled by Mrs. Hussein, or Yugoslavia by Mrs. Milosevic!

To put the potential change in feminine power in the future into the context of life on this planet, here is a history of woman on Earth from Nostradamus's time to today. One of the most notable features of Nostradamus's time was the exclusively autocratic, hierarchical, political and religious structure within Europe, "the great chain of being" on Earth reflecting exactly the view of the divine subscribed to by the Church and State. The old elective kingships of tribal and medieval Europe had long given way to absolute monarchies established by heredity. Succession to the throne was determined by right of primogeniture and consecrated by the Church—the king was "the Lord's anointed." Autocratic rule was thus based upon a partnership between Church and State, with the divine right of kings to govern entrenched in popular belief.

The process was totally male, with God "the Father" handing down his power to the sovereign, who then placed power in the hands of lords, lesser barons, and so on. The father in the home was finally the lord and master of his minirealm, and so the male-dominated social structure flourished. The very few female sovereigns of the day managed to rule through considerable strength and determination, but were actually regarded by society as masculine. The reign of a queen such as Elizabeth I did not produce a matriarchal structure within any social environment, neither in government nor within the family unit. Nor did it produce a balance of power between men and women, or any special form of cooperation or harmony greater than had existed with a king. Men were still in charge, which seemed the natural order of things.

The biblical and popular image of God as a great patriarch in heaven, rewarding and punishing humanity according to his mysterious ways, has dominated the imagination of the Judeo-Christian community for two thousand years. The image of a male "God the Father," first born as a symbol in a patriarchal society and then sustained as plausible by patriarchy until today, has meant that the hierarchical order of both Heaven and Earth was aligned according to an exclusively male order. If God in his heaven is a father ruling his people, then it is according to his divine plan that society on earth by male-dominated.

The mystical relationships between humanity and God, between men and women, reflected this lopsided concept. The images, symbols, and values of this belief system were sustained in Judeo-Christian religion, becoming fixed as "Articles of Faith." In this context, the oppression of women appeared only right and fitting.

The vicious cycle was further exacerbated by the fact that the roles, structures, beliefs, and symbols of this patriarchal society were developed according to an artificial polarization of human qualities into the traditional sexual stereotypes. The masculine universe was seen as objective, aggressive, hyperrational, dominating, manipulating nature and other persons (namely women). The feminine universe was stereotyped as being hyperemotional, passive, and self-abnegating. In this unbalanced view the masculine was safely constant and unchanging; the feminine was mutant and changing, dangerously unpredictable. The universe and its reflection, the world and its inhabitants, were unwisely divided between male and female.

This sex-role segregation of women, which kept them locked in a symbolic ghetto for centuries, was the first stone laid to pave the road to the history of antifeminism. Patriarchal religion first invented and then sustained the dynamics of delusion of such a universe, naming them as "natural," reflective of a divine order, and bestowing supernatural blessings upon them.

There was thus a clear difference between what was "corruptible"—that is, changeable, and therefore feminine—and what was eternal or fixed, and therefore masculine. This fundamental philosophy produced anger and contempt for the world, for the distinction between male and female was the distinction between staying the same and changing.

In Nostradamus's time, and still today, the Moon represented the inconstant (or mutable) as opposed to the fixed and eternal. Anything born under the full Moon, or susceptible to the influence of lunar forces (such as witchcraft or the menstrual cycle) was viewed as suspect. Everything that was removed from lunar influence—such as the Earth (which was seen as the center of the universe), heaven, God—that did not change, was good. Matter, flesh—particularly of the female

variety—was corruptible, while the soul was eternal. Therefore the body was seen as contemptible while the soul,
regarded as masculine, rose after death (the only time of joy)
to join God. No wonder then that Church fathers like Tertullian declared that women "are the devil's gateway," or that
Thomas Aquinas defined women as "misbegotten males."[3]

This conceptual framework formed the basis of male domination, because the center—the soul, God good—was the
power around which everything else—the body, mutability,
femininity—orbited. Obedience was therefore essential, and
the orbiting body of woman had to obey the central power—
man. This was, and still is, men as law.

Patriarchy sustained a view of the universe that was self-
reflective, thus unchangeable, static. For anyone to hint that
this was not so, that the universe had what were erroneously
believed to be "feminine" qualities—that is, that it was mutable and changeable—meant a deviation from the status-quo
belief system. Any such statements and theories were thus
deemed blasphemous.

But at about the time of Nostradamus, there lived another
astronomer and physician who would become a major influence on European thought, whose ideas encapsulated the
New Learning of the Renaissance, and who would open the
way to the power of change and the new feminine spirit. His
name was Nicholas Copernicus.

Copernicus, a Polish astronomer, proposed that the Earth
rotated daily on its axis and orbited the Sun, and not vice
versa. This meant that the Earth was nothing more than one of
several planets traveling around the Sun, which was the center
of the known universe. Copernicus also stated that the uni-

verse in fact went farther than the local system and was, as far as could be divined, infinite. Because of the controversial nature of his findings, his treatise was not published until the year of his death, 1543.

Others then took up this concept and happily developed it, some to their fatal disadvantage. The heretical philosopher Giordano Bruno was burned at the stake for suggesting that the universe was mutable—subject to change, and therefore feminine in nature. Other astronomers suggested that the orbits of the planets were elliptical and not perfect circles—in other words, not the holy, perfect symmetry that the Church had, in its ignorance, positively asserted. Galileo even suggested that the light of the Moon was a reflection of the Sun's rays and that the Sun also moved in an orbit, rather than remaining fixed in one, eternal place.

All this caused no end of embarrassment to the established Church, for it suggested that perhaps the patriarchal model was faulty, to say the least.

Using his powers of divination, his knowledge of astrology based upon the Copernican view of the universe, and ancient alchemical and occult devices, Nostradamus made his own mark on the growing, more open-minded view of the universe. His writings about the future, as we shall see, contain a number of predictions concerning women and their coming powers.

The male, patriarchal worldview was essentially mechanistic in outlook, and continued to remain strong, particularly with the development of classical physics in the Western scientific tradition.

Isaac Newton's universal law of gravitation posited an absolute framework within which forces of attraction acted between separate, rigidly connected bodies. Thus, a force of gravity coming from the Sun acted upon the planets, determining their orbits. After overcoming its resistance to the idea of a heliocentric universe, the Church found comfort in the fixed rigidity of this theory, as it supported a patriarchal view of immutability. But in our own century, scientists such as Einstein and his contemporaries examining the conundrum of quantum mechanics—people like Schrödinger and others—shattered this certainty and brought into play far more complex and "doubtful" theories relating to the absolute and constant presence of the inabsolute and inconstant. They proposed such unlikely and "unpatriarchal" concepts as the fact that subatomic particles can be both waves and particles simultaneously, that they can be both indestructible and destructible, that mass varies with velocity, that man and energy distort space and time, and that time and space are actually connected!

It has even been suggested, via concepts such as Schrödinger's cat-in-the-box paradox, that the very existence of life is no more than the extended vision of human thought patterns, and without the existence of our eyes and our brains, none of this would exist at all! What does this do to the patriarchal need for fixed certainties?[4]

Gazing into his steaming hot, magical, changing, divining bowl, Nostradamus foresaw the end of arid male rationalism.

The New Balance of the Feminine

One of the most pervasive characteristics of the patriarchal status quo is its dependence on division, on the differences between things as opposed to the similarities they share. Where differences arise, so superiorities and inferiorities are born. The whole basis of this concept of duality—right and wrong, black and white, good and bad, man and woman—is male in origin and naturally gives rise to the corollary of one being either legally or morally better than the other. There are even remaining associations in the twenty-first century that perpetuate the distinctions, for example between left and right. This state of opposites can be seen in such bizarre differences as the way we button our shirts! Men's shirts button on the right, women's on the left. At a wedding ceremony the groom's party sits on the right and the bride's on the left. This custom derives from what we now call superstitions from the past, but which at the time of their inception were considered seriously, even medically, and certainly religiously, as facts of life. Jesus sat on the right hand of God, and during banquets and feasts, even everyday meals, the favored child, probably the son, or a good friend, would sit on the right side of the "man of the house." The devil always stands on the left shoulder of the unfortunate sinner, which is why we throw salt over the left shoulder to blind him. We mostly write with the right hand, not the left, and left-handed people tend to be thought of as a little different, or perhaps eccentric. In medical science, during very early parts of this century, it was believed that semen from the right testicle produced boys and that from the left, girls. It is notable that the part of the women in this "decision" was seemingly not relevant. Men determined everything.

However, when it comes to the brain, matters concerned with left and right go sadly wrong. The left side of the brain, according to modern medicine, performs those logical,

ordered, and linear functions of our lives, while the right has a
holistic point of view and performs activities requiring intu-
ition, creativity, and visualization. And the "crowning" discovery is that the best results are achieved from learning to coor-
dinate the sides equally, so that a balance is found in our daily
lives. Modern psychology, and particularly the spiritual
philosophies derived from a greater exposure to Eastern,
especially Indian, concepts, preach the basic necessity of inte-
gration, of bringing the male and female within each of us to
bear on all life's demands. But first, according to Nostradamus, the feminine must reach a higher peak of power.

With a view to exploring this progress we begin with one
of the verses quoted at the beginning of this section, in which
Nostradamus's words tell us much more than at first appears.

> *A new law will emerge in the new world of America,*
> *at a time when Syria, Judea and Palestine*
> *are significant:*
> *the great barbarian empire of patriarchy that men*
> *have created will decay during the time that the*
> *feminine spirit is completing its cycle.*

Nostradamus expresses his meaning through extremely
economical language. The first line directs us to the location
of this new law. To sixteenth-century Europeans, the mythical
attributes and untapped potential of the New World were a
powerful magnet. Throughout his verses Nostradamus frequently refers to "the new land" to mean America. This is an
established interpretation, and in this case the "new law" that
will arise there is related, in the last two lines, to two factors—

the existence of a "barbarian" male empire, which is in decay, which is in turn related to the Moon and its cycles—a common metaphorical association with woman. Put simply, the great virgin territories of the New World will be the source of a rising "lunar" consciousness at a time when Judeo-Christian tradition is at its peak—the brute rule of patriarchy will start to crumble before the female evolution is complete. This is the beginning of our story, and the position that humanity has reached at the beginning of the twenty-first century.

Nostradamus foresaw democracy as a force in human affairs that would supersede the autocratic monarchies of his day. These, he predicted, would thus be gradually replaced or replenished by a greater female influence, producing in its turn an entirely new world order. This process is the fundamental theme of this section of the book, as we see the prediction of the accretion of a "critical mass" of feminine power unfold within the prophet's verses.

As an underlying feature of women's position in society, and as a part of Nostradamus's predicted "new law," which we can take quite literally as referring to the legal aspects of society, we shall see changes, for example, in institutions such as the criminal and civil justice systems of the United States and European countries; these will facilitate greater female equality and give women an increasingly important position during the first years of this millennium and in the next few decades.

In order for women to be able to function independently of male influence, it already, during the 1990s, became apparent that in the established judicial processes with regard to women's rights there were major holes that needed to be blocked. Areas of criminal and civil law such as those governing rape, sexual abuse, and marital abuse are the subject of heated debate, and there were more court cases surrounding these aspects of the law in the 1990s than ever before in history. Within the more militant sectors of the women's liberation movement there is still a sense of anger against "sexist" institutions, particularly in America, where attitudes against male domination are growing stronger every year.

Male-dominated institutions from the political arena all the way to the Roman Catholic Church are finding themselves under attack, and there has already been a considerable growth of female power in many sectors. According to the book *Megatrends for Women* by Patricia Aburdene and John Naisbitt:[5]

> In 1993, 38 percent of the House of Representatives legislature in Washington were women.

> In the United States there were, in 1993, more than 5 million female-owned businesses, which contributed more jobs than the whole of the Fortune 500 companies put together.[6]

One of the most important messages within the quatrains is that there will come a time, at the beginning of this millennium, when a critical mass of female power will occur. The timing of this change is established by the fact that Nostradamus makes frequent reference to the "new world" or "new country," meaning America, as being the catalyst for such change. The United States has become a Super Power only in the last half of the last century.

The concept of "critical mass" was formulated first in physics, which defined it as the minimum quantity of radioactive material needed to produce a nuclear chain reaction. In human terms, a critical mass may occur in a social environment where dissatisfaction grows to a level where revolution occurs, simply through the gathering of enough angry people all in one place, all with sufficient energy to force change. The surrounding environmental and social response to this catalyst also plays a part in the size and shape of the resulting new paradigm. Once this critical mass has reached its peak, the result is a self-sustaining change. Paradigm shifts occur in this way. As we shall see in this chapter, Nostradamus's verses can be interpreted to predict the formation of a critical mass of women with a militant march across Europe.

According to the verses quoted below, a large group of women will take a militant stand in order to effect major changes within contemporary society. We may feel that this has already happened during the 1980s and early 1990s, with militant feminism playing a strong part in helping to shift the stubborn male domain, but according to this interpretation of Nostradamus there is more to come, or in truth the patriarchal format still dominates the civilized world. First come the literal translations of the verses, and then there follows a more free interpretation.

From the shore of Lake Garda to Lake Fucino,
Taken from the Lake of Geneva to the port of
*   "L'Orguion":*
Born of three arms the predated warlike image,
Through three crowns to great Endymium.

From Sens, from Autun they will come as far as
  the Rhone
To pass beyond and towards the Pyrenees
    mountains:
The nation to leave the march at Ancona:
By land and sea it will be followed by great trails.

  The voice of the unusual bird is heard
On the pipe (or canon) of the floor
So high will come from the wheat the bushel
That man will be a cannibal to man.

  Lightning in Burgundy will make something
    portentous,
One which could never have happened through skill,
A sexton made lame by the senate
Will inform the enemy of the matter:

  Thrown back because of bows, fires, pitch and
    more fire:
Cries, shouts are heard at midnight:
Inside they are put onto broken battlements,
The traitors fled by underground passageways.

  Great Neptune from the deep sea
With Punic forms mixed with Gallic blood,
The Isles bleed, because of the late rowing:
More harm will it do to him, the badly conceived
    secret.

  The beard sizzled and black because of skill
Will reduce the cruel and proud people:
The great Chyren will remove from far away
All those captured by the banner of Selin.

  After the conflict by the eloquence of the one that is
    wounded

For a short while a false rest is managed:
The great ones are not to be allowed to be delivered
    at all
They are returned by the enemy at the right time.
  Through fire from the sky the city is almost
    burned:
The Urn threatens Deucalion again:
Sardina made angry by the Punic foist,
After Libra will leave her Phaethon.
  Through hunger the prey will make the wolf
    prisoner;
The aggressor then in extreme distress.
The heir having the last one before him,
The great one does not escape in the middle of the
    crowd.

                 —C2 V73–82[7]

These are among the most fascinating of all the quatrains in the *Centuries*, particularly as they seem to form a story running longer than any other series of verses appearing to refer to one event. It can be inferred from this that the event described—a march of women, under the *banner of Seline* (the Moon goddess Selene) across the power centers of Europe—is one of the most significant in history. And although during the early twenty-first century some may not expect there to be a need for still greater feminine militancy, there is little doubt in the author's mind that it is time that the patriarchal system fell by the wayside. Previous societies, pre-Sumerian, pre-Egyptian, early European, have lived by different codes, without the domination, competitiveness, and aggressiveness of the modern world, and they have been shown through recent anthropological discoveries to have lived more happily and with less misery than ourselves. As we shall see in the coming pages, Nostradamus foresaw a similar world to those ancient, peaceful, nonpatriarchal societies, returning to Earth through the influence of woman.

So perhaps we can first "free-interpret" the lines of these verses to examine more closely where the prediction leads us.

From the shore of Lake Garda (in northeastern Italy) to the former Lake Fucino (now drained, an area of land sixty-five miles east of Rome) moving from Lake Geneva (in Switzerland) to the port of the Orgueil (to be discussed later) born out of three labors according to a predicted warlike image through three wreaths to the great lover of the Moon (Endymion, son of Zeus, was the lover of Selene, goddess of the Moon).

From Sens (northeast France, then in the Duchy of Burgundy) and Autun (also in Burgundy, one hundred miles from Sens) they will come as far as from the River Rhone to travel as far as the Pyrenees mountains, of those arising in Italy, a group of people will leave the march at Ancona (east coast of Italy); by land and sea it will be followed by great trails.

A big, unusual bird (possibly a bird of prey or a symbol) will be high in the sky where the air is still breathable; down near the earth is a layer that is not breathable, where men live and a famine exists, making men cannibals.

Powers in Burgundy will inflict punishment on
the people of the march, and this will be told to the
marchers by a disempowered cleric serving the
State. They will be repelled by fire and weapons with
cries heard at midnight and traitors to the cause
will escape through underground passages.

Forces (probably military or police) from the
Ottoman Empire and France (a fundamentalist
backlash) will stand against the march, coming
from the sea, though because of a late start will fail
to stop it.

Men (bearded), burned by the skill of the
marchers, will fight and beat them cruelly. The great
comet Chiron will be seen moving far away by all
those under the banner of Seline.

After the conflict an eloquent individual who was
wounded secures a truce, which proves to be false,
for the rest of the marchers, while those leaders who
were captured by the enemy (presumably men) are
returned at the right time.

Because of bombs or rockets a city nearby is
burned: the son of the creator of mankind
(Deucalion was the son of Prometheus, the creator of
mankind in Greek mythology, whose task it was to
renew the human race) is threatened again and the
conflict is made worse by involvement from the
people of Sardinia, which, after Libra (an
astrological reference) will leave her Phaethon (a
mythological reference to be explained).

Because of a yearning the women will make the

*men prisoners, so that they are very distressed. Even
if the new heir (woman) stands behind the great one
(man), she will now be noticed.*

In translating and interpreting these complex and fascinating lines, we have used a number of devices:

Local historical references and symbols that have some connection with the lifetime and locations of Nostradamus himself. In the author's previous book—*Nostradamus: The Millennium and Beyond*—it was suggested that Nostradamus used his own period of history, including people and locations, as metaphors for events in the future.[8]

Mythological symbolism from the distant past—such as Greek mythological heroes like Phaethon.

A knowledge of history as it has developed up to the twenty-first century—in other words, we are aware that there is a growing feminist movement and have therefore applied this knowledge to the verses.

Employing the above methods the outlines of a story are revealed, of a march of women across Europe involving a large part of Italy, Switzerland, and France, initially to establish rights that have not been granted to them, but evolving into a very significant event on the global scene. These rights may well concern equality, money, and effectiveness in society, and by the tone of the overall prediction, this is a major event also in the history of womankind. The march undertaken, presumably by a large number of women, derives from a number of starting points: northern Italy, the area of Rome, from Switzerland near Lake Geneva, and an area that is given the title. "L'Orguion," which is interpreted by Edgar Leoni (one of the most prosaic and intelligent interpreters of Nostradamus) to refer to the town of Orgon, twenty miles north of Salon, where Nostradamus lived, and which was, perhaps either coincidentally or significantly, an area where in 1864 a meteorite fell.[9] This meteorite was found to contain elements of carbon, seeds, reed, and other fragments, indicating the presence of life in another part of the universe. On closer examination it became clear that these items had been embedded there deliberately, in an attempt to create a hoax. This reference may have some significance once the march of Seline Movement occurs.

Something that needs to be understood about Nostradamus's visions is that very often scenes and concepts, words and facts might be given to him that made little sense even to him, so that we are interpreting something that can only ultimately be verified when and if it actually occurs.

In the free interpretation we see that the movement is born out of three labors and a "predicted warlike image" of three wreaths, under the lovers of Engymion, whom we connect through mythology with the Moon. It is said that Nostradamus himself was unable to interpret this enigmatic verse, though there are those in his future (the interpreter Allen, who wrote in 1943) who believe it refers to America because of the mythological connection between Engymion and Selene, who put him into a perpetual slumber so that she could caress him at will.[10] Why this should be seen as a metaphor for the United States is something of a mystery, unless we believe that in the context of feminism, the United States is asleep to the feminine spirit, or else that man has put women to sleep so that he may caress her without making love to her.

A more likely explanation is that the banner carried by the women of the Seline Movement contains symbols of labor and three victors' wreaths that have some significance at the time, and this war-like image associated with the Moon is clearly another symbolic reference to the need for an aggressive and powerful stance by women to achieve their ends. The Moon as symbol of womanhood is clear.

The story continues, telling us which regions the marchers will come from and where they will all march to—converging, it seems, on Ancona, on the eastern coast of Italy.

We then read of conditions that sound extreme, to say the least. High in the sky the air is breathable, whereas close to the ground the atmosphere is polluted and men suffer from famine (in the original, Nostradamus refers to the pipe of the air vent floor, an extraordinary piece of twenty-first-century description for a sixteenth-century writer). Nostradamus has a habit of expressing things in an extreme way, but if we consider how our own time would have looked from his vantage point—before the Industrial Revolution, when air was pure, when motor vehicles were unknown and rivers and oceans were still free from pollution—it might well seem to him that our air was not breathable, and that we were suffering from famine. It could also be that he was not necessarily referring to famine in Italy, but in other parts of the world, thus giving us a time frame to date the prediction.

In effect, this Seline Movement, and the march across Europe, are linked to the modern Industrial Age and could therefore occur at any time in the latter years of this century.

We then receive some details of hostile local governments (the Burgundians, in the previous century, had captured Joan of Arc and handed her over to the English for trial) and of escapes through underground passages, together with political and military forces (*Punic forces mixed with Gallic blood*, which is both Christian and Islamic) being deployed to prevent the march from progressing.

This march will, incidentally, be the first to occur across several borders, a truly international revolutionary march. Its route, perhaps coincidentally, according to Nostradamus's description, traces in reverse Hannibal's march against Rome in 218 B.C. during the Second Punic War—traveling over the Alps, down the Rhone Valley into southern France and then to Spain—somehow signifying a reversal of historical process. The journey from Rome to Carthage can be seen as a return to the early Mediterranean religion.

In the sky, during the march of the Seline Movement, the comet Chiron will be seen passing overhead. Chiron is an old and regular "friend" of planet Earth. During the 1970s it was thought to be another planet moving in an unstable orbit between Saturn and Uranus, but after a dust envelope was detected around its orbit in the 1980s it was reclassified as a comet.[11]

Nostradamus is very keen on comets, which crop up frequently in his predictions. Because of their cyclical nature, they are a useful device for timing events in the future. Why he should have chosen Chiron to be the comet seen by the women of the Seline Movement is a mystery, because it is not generally visible in the night sky without the help of a powerful telescope; so there may be another reason for this reference. It could be that he was telling us to look at both the comet Chiron and at the mythological associations of its name, in order to give some idea of when this event will take place. We discover, if we look into Greek mythology, that Chiron was a wise Centaur who, after being wounded, was transformed by the gods into the constellation Sagittarius, which lies between Scorpio and Capicorn in the Zodiac. The Sun passes through Sagittarius from November to December, up to the winter solstice (December 21/22), so we can infer that the march will take place at this time of year. Unfortunately, Chiron, in the course of its solar orbit, is only occasionally visible on Earth, when it happens to be lit by the Sun's rays, and we cannot therefore predict a year when this might occur.

The story continues with details of a deal made by one who is wounded and eloquent, which fails, but which results in the return of prisoners.

The conflict created by these marchers appears to be on a large scale, for we are next informed of bombs, rickets, and a burned city, with involvement by the people of the island of Sardinia, provoked by the *Punic foist*—the spiritual return to Carthage.

Here we are given a typical Nostradamus reference, combining astrology and ancient mythology.

It takes the form of three separate, though connected, references:

Deucalion

After Libra

Phaëthon

Deucalion, King of Phthia, was the son of Prometheus, the Titan who created human beings and gave them fire, in Greek mythology. Like Noah, Deucalion survived a Flood, let loose by Zeus, in an ark—a moonship, the Mesopotamian version. His task was to renew the human race after its fall, an important metaphor, for Nostradamus sees the evolution of woman as being highly significant in the rebirth of humanity.[12]

The reference to *after Libra* indicates both a planetary movement and a metaphorical reference to justice. Libra represents the scales of justice, perhaps going to another indication of the Prophet's view of women's ideal place in the balance of society. In astrological terms it lies between Virgo and Scorpio, and the Sun passes through Libra during October. *After Libra* takes us to the December/January period in which the comet Chiron returns to our skies. It is as though we are receiving a detailed timeline of the progress of the march. We then learn of a connection with Phaëthon.

Phaëthon is the Greek word for shining, or radiant. In Greek mythology Phaëthon was the son of the Sun god, Helios, and the nymph Rhode. Phaëthon plagued his father to allow him to drive the chariot of the Sun through the heavens for a single day. His wish was granted, but Phaëthon was unable to control the horses and the chariot traveled first so high that everyone shivered, and then so close to the earth that he scorched it. To prevent severe damage Zeus struck him with a thunderbolt, causing him to fall into the Eridanu (Po) river. He was mourned by his sisters, Prote and Clymene, who turned into poplar trees on the banks, weeping amber tears.[13]

The reference reiterates that the Sun is in the astrological house of Libra. The allegorical aspect of these words emphasizes that men will be brought low through their folly. All this apparently takes place in the months December/January of the year that Chiron becomes visible from Earth.

The last paragraph rounds off the story by telling us that whatever occurs in this mighty stand by women, the result will be an undeniable, greater presence of the feminine spirit in the world. If we accept this interpretation of the verses, the march by a group called "Seline" is one of the pivotal features of women's evolution, which will develop a militant format in the coming years and will push feminine power and equality further along the road, so forming the central core of the feminine critical mass.

We may presume this, then, to be a very significant event in our future.

2009 WOMEN AT THE TOP

With a name so timid will she be brought forth
That the three sisters will have the name of destiny:
Then she will lead a great people by tongue and deed,
More than any other will she have fame and renown.
    —C1 V76[1]

It is proposed that this quatrain applies to the events resulting from the "revolt" on the part of women of the Seline Movement. A free interpretation of the verse follows:

The timid name of woman will be dispelled and she
will be raised up to greater importance. The three
sisters of womanhood (a classical reference to be
explained) will find their place in destiny: then she
will lead a great people by word and deed, and more
than any other will she have fame and renown.

Put simply, womankind had, previous to the Seline Movement, been associated with weakness, at least in the eyes of men. But not before time, she will be raised to much greater heights of importance. Here again we see the number three

applied to the women's movement, a number previously
encountered in the long story related to the Seline Movement,
and which we shall see again when we look at how the future
develops as a result of it. The three sisters in this case are alle-
gorized from classical mythology and refer to the three ages of
woman—virgin, mother, and old woman. The "Triple Goddess" is referred to in *The Great Cosmic Mother* by Monica
Sjöö and Barbara Mor.

> *The moon, as daughter of the Great Mother, is known
> as the Triple Goddess. She presides over all acts of
> generation, whether physical, intellectual, or
> spiritual. Her triple aspect expresses the three
> phases of the moon: waxing (growth), full (rebirth)
> and waning (periodic death).*
>
> *She is, as the New or Waxing Moon, the white
> Goddess of birth and growth.*
>
> *She is, as the Full Moon, the Red Goddess of love
> and battle.*
>
> *She is, as the Old or Waning Moon, the Black
> Goddess of death and divination.*
>
> *These are the three phases of the woman life, all
> natural and all magical.*[2]

This reference helps us to understand the concept that
Nostradamus was perhaps trying to portray in this verse—the
renewed presence of woman as the center of magic in the
world. The last line of the verse reaffirms that woman will play
a much stronger part in leading the world and will enjoy great
fame and fortune.

The first and most obvious areas in which this new power is likely to be felt are in the State and Church, and in his use of words such as "destiny" and "fame and renown" we can interpret Nostradamus as hinting at the increasing likelihood of women acceding to positions of power in government—women such as Margaret Thatcher, Hillary Clinton, Ann Richards (until recently governor of Texas), and Barbara Boxer (California senator). This applies to women in other countries around the world—to Violeta Chamorro, who defeated Daniel Ortega to lead Nicaragua in 1990; in Brazil, to Luiza Eurndina de Souza, mayor of São Paulo; in Japan, to Sadako Ogata, Japan's highest-ranking official at the United Nations; in the Philippines, to Corazón Aquino; in Pakistan, to Benazir Bhutto, once prime minister; in Russia, to Larisa Kuznetsova and Tatyana Ivanova, currently heads of the Moscow Women's Political Club. All these women are part of what will eventually be the norm throughout the world, the first step toward the critical mass of feminist political power. Then there is the presence of women in the established churches, whom we will examine more closely later in the book.[3]

One of the other areas that women will, of course, have an increasing impact on is in the business arena. Figures quoted in *Megatrends for Women* by Patricia Aburdene and John Naisbitt show that during 1977 there were only 2 million female-owned businesses in the United States, turning over revenues of $25 billion. By 1988 there were 5 million female-owned businesses, with revenues of over $83 billion. During that eleven-year period independent businesses overall increased revenues by some 56 percent.[4] According to figures published in various U.S. economic journals, this trend is continuing and increasing in a giant exponential curve in the early part of the new millennium, contributing enormously to the general critical mass of the feminine spirit.[5]

In order to establish a time line for future predictions, it is necessary to place a date, even if it is slightly random, upon the start of what we would call the feminist movement. The most obvious era would be the 1960s, when women really began to stand up and be counted; but for that matter we could also date it much earlier, for during the first years of this century Emmeline Pankhurst was responsible for winning women the vote, so perhaps this entire period of history right up to today should really be considered to be the prelude to the true feminine revolution. This view is certainly consistent with the predictions we are examining, and with the general interpretation of this book. For the sense of the prophecies is that women's liberation has really only just begun.

In *Megatrends for Women* Patricia Aburdene and John Naisbitt state:

> *This book takes women's liberation as a point of departure and asks, What comes next?*

We therefore suggest that the real women's movement only began in the early 1990s, and this will act as our point of departure for any dates and times given in Nostradamus's quatrains.

Still more fundamental to the fortunes of women is their growing influence over love and the family. Though there has been, during the past few decades, a powerful swing toward feminism and a greater equality of the sexes, Nostradamus indicates that the years of determination, culminating in a final militant mass march, result ultimately in female predominance both in the world at large and within the family at home.

In the quatrain at the beginning of this section we find a prediction related to the dwindling of male power—*Iron will cool*—at the hands of the female *wound*. Nostradamus seems to be pointing to the likelihood of positive changes occurring once the concept of "feminine energy" becomes better understood in the hitherto male-dominated world—once the *banner of Seline* has been established following the march across Europe.

The result of our critical mass for change, however, is not simply the replacement of male dominance by female, but a completely new paradigm of men and women finding their full potential in cooperation with one another. During the latter years of the twentieth century the pendulum, presently moving away from the point in the arc that had kept men in power, swings more rapidly to the other side, where female power is felt more urgently. During the twenty-first century it settles near the center, finding a more cooperative and relaxed atmosphere between the sexes.

A free interpretation of the quatrain at the beginning to this section might tell us more:

Woman has been hidden behind deep shadows; her
brother, man, has moved through the world with
hardness and heaviness, eclipsing her for so long.
But this hot, iron-like property of man will cool in
the feminine spirit that grows around him.

What is becoming rapidly more evident in the last years of the early years of the twenty-first century are the changes that occur when men are transformed by an overwhelming presence of feminine energy. Humanity has spent many thousands of years at war, striving to improve its material welfare and battling it out between nations and beliefs. As a result, man has damaged his world almost to the point of rendering it beyond repair. If we believe what Nostradamus tells us, then the time has now come for a very different kind of energy to patch up and transform the strife-torn world.

In the first years of the new millennium there might still be those who insist that the presence of a "stronger woman," the form of the feminist movement, merely changes the players in an unchanging drama—the same roles are assumed by different players who happen to be female in character but are still essentially operating in the traditional male way. This idea is based on the fact that women who presently occupy "masculine" positions, such as those in politics or religion, seem to behave like men!

In effect, the fact that there are still so few women in what can easily be observed to be "male" jobs somehow preserves the stereotypes rather than transforms them. We might call their presence "tokenism," and tokenism certainly reduces any revolutionary drive for transformation, for it is simply drowned out by the overwhelmingly stronger male energy that exists around it.

In the United States, for example, the tiny numbers of women who are judges, chief executive officers of large corporations, doctors, or politicians have often been trained by men in organizations and schools designed and completely influenced by men and their male energy. These women must, in some part at least, have been shaped or influenced by this male-dominated pressure.

What Nostradamus is telling us in this verse, it is suggested, is that masculine energy will literally be dulled by the overwhelming presence of women in positions of influence and power, but only once a female consciousness has developed. Only at the point when this occurs will there be a major transformation of energy in this world, and a resulting change.

It is certainly quite wrong to assume that the feminine movement will somehow only create a race of women willing to accept the existing beliefs, structures, and patterns of male society. The transformation caused by the presence of women will strike at the very roots of the male society that has been the norm up to the present time. The transformation that we are about to witness, in the lifetimes of most of us, is a complete rejection of patriarchal values, which will result in the total replacement of those values with something completely different.

Feminine Shockwave

The new paradigm of a greater female balance within the world will need very careful management, and a difficult transition occurred over the years from 1997 to 2004 when the presence of women in important positions both in world affairs and within the home was the determining factor in the change. We may imagine that the world can handle a growing feminine energy, but most civilized countries have been dominated by men for several thousand years and various fundamental structures will alter when they cease to be in command. This change will occur most violently in countries that are still dominated by patriarchal attitudes such as those inherent in parts of the Middle East where religion totally opposes the feminine spirit.

A basic human "habit" will be dismantled during this era of change, so that underlying emotional, practical, and political changes will form part of a massive experience of human renewal. This basic, underlying shift will give rise to transformations and changes in aspects of life such as science and technology, invention and innovation, creativity in the arts, birth, child-care methods and education, medicine, and the role of the aged as elders of local communities.

A free interpretation of the verse at the top of this section might be:

The change caused by the powerful presence of the female will be very difficult: but the whole world will gain by the change. The heart will be the most important feature of this transformation, but also prudence will be as much an established aspect of this new life, chasing out the cunning created by man. The entire world, in all aspects, will be altered in the most fundamental way.

The earliest visible cracks that are being seen in the massive and ancient edifice of patriarchy have occurred already in the early 1990s with judicial confrontations such as the Mike Tyson and William Kennedy Smith rape trials, and particularly the Anita Hill hearings in 1991, in which members of the U.S.

Senate were seriously unhinged by allegations of sexual harassment.

The main feature of these cases was the evident lack of understanding, and even wild anger, among white men in authority at the suggestion that women might have a completely different view of reality from that of the patriarchal establishment. The pitiful lack of female representation in government in the United States and throughout most of the rest of the civilized world has now become an issue to the female population as a result of such confrontations, for they not only highlight women's lack of real power in the world, but they also reveal the true nature of male authority.

What has developed from this often necessarily aggressive stance of women in America is literally a "genderquake"— which Nostradamus's predictions echo through into the twenty-first century. This can most readily be seen in the progress made by President Clinton's preelection campaign and the power given it by the presence of Hillary Clinton. She stands not only as a powerful female personality backing the male power position, but as an empowered individual, a lawyer in her own right, opposed to the relatively nonfeminist position that had by contrast been taken by Barbara Bush while President Bush was in power and by Mrs. Bush Jr. during George Bush's very male presidency. Political commentators during the time of Clinton's presidency implied that the elections that put him into the White House with the Democratic party behind him were won because of the lack of understanding within the Republican party of the political importance of the female genderquake.

A formative influence in this new move toward greater

feminine consciousness was the media, spearheaded by the Oprah Winfrey show, which constantly undermines patriarchal values by bringing destructive male influences in the family to the forefront of American TV viewing. Women have become aware that they can actually speak about their needs and attitudes and tell the stories of their degradation and disadvantage to a massive and listening public, including women who still choose to remain within the conventional role of "housewife."

The most interesting aspect of Nostradamus's verses lies in his frequent references to the presence of the heart in the affairs of women in the future. Probably the single most powerful force that the feminine influence will bring, according to this interpretation of the Prophet's works, is that ultimately women will discard "cunning" and the old, very often dishonest, political methods that patriarchy has given rise to, in favor of honest, truthful, and loving ways of relating in the world.

And the change is taking place not only in the United States but throughout many other parts of the world.

In the United Kingdom, the Conservative government under the leadership of Tony Blair has been forced into providing greater opportunities for women in senior public positions by considering such devices as a Citizens' Charter for women; and there was even a suggestion by one of the earlier Labor party leaders that there could be a Ministry for Women, something that in the future will no doubt be considered a normal requirement of governments everywhere.[6]

The reason for all this, of course, is not a sudden shift in the attitude of the politicians occurring because of an intrinsic change of *gestalt*, but simply because they have been forced into an awareness of the number of female votes "out there" that might unseat them if they don't comply. And it will be in this way that the political, and incidentally probably the religious, attitudes will develop toward what Nostradamus indicates in his predictions for the near future.

In Australia, women's issues are being taken increasingly seriously. Within the Australian workforce, according to figures quoted in Naomi Wolf's book *Fire with Fire*, women accounted for 41 percent.[7] In addition she relates that 33 percent of small businesses in that country are owned by women. As a result of acknowledging the needs that arise from such evident dramatic growth in the influence of women in Australian society, Paul Keating won the election in 1991.[8]

Norway enjoys a woman prime minister, with seven of the seventeen ministers being women, and half of the total police force too—a staggering change in the overall condition of the country's political and power regime resulting. The same sort of picture can be seen developing in Turkey, Spain, Sweden, and Uganda, where women's issues have created a feminine awareness in the political arena through the determined emergence of female voters.[9]

With the rapid growth of global awareness, and the reduction in political suppression that has occurred since the end of communism in the Baltic countries, activities and changes in countries like the United States have become visible to a vast audience through television. The whole world will become increasingly aware of transformation in America and Europe in the future, so that as the world's leading and most advanced countries "get it together" to have women represented effectively, and as patriarchal values become more obviously ineffective, so the global trend will move in the same direction. In this way the feminine earthquake will grow in strength as we begin the last century of male domination.

Changes in Education

In *Megatrends for Women*, Patricia Aburdene and John Naisbitt indicate that one of the other most important areas of change— which falls within the arena of "difficulty" that Nostradamus sees as necessary and fundamental to the growth of female awareness—will be in basic education systems, which will lead to the new paradigm of feminine equality and cooperation. Within the traditional education of the average boy at school, there has been an emphasis on the patriarchal values of achievement, independence, competitiveness, and self-sufficiency, whereas for the young girl, the emphasis has always been on dependence (or codependence), cooperation, group orientation, and home economics.

These forms of conditioning naturally tend to produce results that fit in with the social requirements of "man as bread winner" and "woman as homemaker and childbearer." And it is these fundamental indoctrinations that Nostradamus indicates will change. Expectations will be similar for both sexes, but there will also be a much greater emphasis on individual education, fashioned in each case for special needs.

She-God

In recent years many more divine visions of the Virgin Mary have been recorded throughout the world. Within the Catholic

Church, and indeed from the Vatican itself, there is already some excitement about the idea that these increasingly frequent "visitations" signify a kind of "Second Coming" in the form of spiritual guidance within the Catholic tradition. It is interesting to note that the visions are always significantly feminine. One of the most famous examples is the visions of the children in Medjugorje, in the former Yugoslavia, where the Virgin Mary appeared to the children every evening for several years. It is perhaps significant that she appeared just before the beginning of the war that split Yugoslavia into religious factions.[10]

There are literally hundreds of other examples around the world, and we may take these either to be the Catholic "Mother of God" specifically, or perhaps, in a broader sense, the returning presence of the ancient Mother Goddess who was said to watch over humanity in pre-Christian times.

In any event, given the human tendency to make manifest its most important myths and symbols, we may understand the increase in such apparitions to be related to the human need for a holy female presence.

Nostradamus indicates to us that during the coming decades woman's increasing importance within the established Churches and other sects does not simply signify a few women priests, but a radical change in the world view of religion and of the need for feminine remedies. In order for this to come about, women are going to overturn thousands of years of the most sexist tradition of them all—challenging the authority of the male churches, reinterpreting the Bible, gaining ordination as a matter of course, and generally integrating feminine concepts into general religious understanding.

This includes some very fundamental attitudes, and certainly a radical new look at male-dominated Fundamentalist movement in the United States.

We may now expect a new religious understanding to occur in our near future related to personal godliness, involving literally a "She-God," which redefines the meaning of love and holiness. Interpreted freely, the quatrain at the beginning of this chapter might read as follows:

Within the most fundamental aspects of the world which is affected by the presence of religion, a holy feminine presence will be heard as a gentle but important voice. This very human flame will be seen to shine in a divine light. Its presence will cause the world and all who live in it to be changed in a fundamental way which will include the death of the dominance of male religious influence . . .

This presence will destroy the established Churches of the male-dominated religious forces.

This very subtle piece of prophetic writing began with a reference to the visions of a Mother Goddess. And perhaps we may use this opportunity to go back, far back, into history, to a time long before patriarchal values were even considered. It may sound unlikely to modern man and woman, so entrenched in patriarchy as we are, that there actually was a time when attitudes engendered by competitiveness, domination, and prejudice did not exist at all.

The Ancient Essence

One of the characteristics of any individual personality is that she or he will view the world through the eyes of that personality. If you are an angry person, you will see the world as angry. If you are loving and simple, you will see the world as loving and simple. We are, in a sense, walking projectionists, beaming our inner aspects onto the screen of the world.

So also, we do this as whole civilizations. We are a competitive, male-oriented, dominating, aggressive society, and we tend to see the past through these eyes—often quite wrongly. Thus tombs opened in Egypt, containing elaborate burial chambers, were assumed to be those of kings, but they turned out to be the tombs of the mothers of kings, the king himself being given lesser place.

According to quite recent discoveries, there have been successful societies in our distant past that were not patriarchal, aggressive, and competitive. One such is the civilization of Minoan Crete, discovered by Sir Arthur Evans in the opening decades of this century.[11]

Excavations on Crete between 1930 and 1980 have yielded greater detail about this socially complex and technologically advanced ancient society. In her book *The Chalice and the Blade*, Riane Eisler describes evidence of huge multistoried palaces, homes and farms, well-organized cities, and road networks. Four forms of language and writing were found— Hieroglyphic, Proto-linear, Linear A, and Linear B, which in archeological terms places Minoan society in a much more recent, historic (as opposed to prehistoric) stage of develop-

ment than its period would suggest. It is evident that this was
no ordinary, traditional civilization.[12]

The archeologist Nicolas Platon, who had excavated in
Crete for almost fifty years by 1980, uncovered a civilization
that had begun before 6000 B.C.[13] A small group of people from
southwest Asia Minor had settled on the island, bringing with
them the traditions of the Goddess cult, a view of life that pre-
vailed throughout the Neolithic period. Their social and technological skills continued to develop for four thousand years,
until around 2000 B.C.E., when Crete entered the Middle
Menoan period—well into the Bronze Age, a time when the
partnership concept of society, worshipping the Goddess cult,
was being replaced by war-like, essentially male gods. In all
the discoveries made on Crete there are no signs of war, even
up to the fifteenth century B.C.E., when the Minoan culture was
destroyed. The essential feature of the worship of the Goddess
was what Joseph Campbell called "syncretism."[14] Put in other
words, her worship was both monotheistic and polytheistic.
Modern monotheistic religions such as Christianity, Islam, and
Buddhism limit themselves to a God who is both male and
exclusive. The Crean and Neolithic religion was based upon a
Mother Goddess who took many different forms in different
civilizations but who put people in touch with nature, and was
the focus of a widespread human understanding of nature as
one entity. This extraordinary unity between humanity and its
environment probably originally arose out of the prehistoric
need to "live off the land." The nourishing Earth was the
source of birth, life, and death to those who depended upon it.
Prehistoric people depended first on the annual migrations of
the animals, and then more directly on the cycles of the land,

the seasons, and the harvest, and quite naturally regarded the Earth as the source or mother of all existence.

The source was seen as essentially female in character. Thus the feminine spirit was born and became ruler of all she surveyed.

When modern feminists speak of God as a woman, this is perhaps their source, and indeed it is a much more realistic focus than any male symbol. The male God was born only out of a war-like, aggressive, and competitive ethos that destroyed the Mother Goddess and literally took over the world in the Iron Age, causing the rise of large and mutually hostile empires based on conquest. This set the pattern of war and conflict between nations for the next three thousand years. Thus modern civilizations can be said to have provided largely misery and little else, other than perhaps the growth of the industrialized world, which in the light of the harmony enjoyed by ancient civilizations such as that of Crete might seem to have been a mistake.

In any event, the central religious image of the Neolithic world, which was later echoed in Crete, was that of woman giving rather than man dying on a cross. We could say that this is the contrast between the love of life and the fear of death. We could also hope that we might abandon the one and return to the other, and Nostradamus's verses give us the direct impression that the rebirth of the feminine spirit is the single biggest step toward that return to joy. But it is not, so far as can be interpreted from the prophet's works, a matter of changing from patriarchy to matriarchy—this would be only a switch of players while the game stays the same. The reasoning that comes to the conclusion that if patriarchal values are not present then matriarchal values must replace them is based on the assumption of domination. But domination is a male concept and will not necessarily exist in the postpatriarchal society we can envisage with the help of Nostradamus's verses.

Evidence presented in various studies, for example those undertaken by James Mellaart of the British Institute of Archeology at Ankara into prepatriarchal Neolithic societies, shows more advanced and stable cultures worshipping within the Goddess's religious structures.[15] These structures bore no resemblance to the dominant patriarchal cultures of the last millennia and yet were entirely peaceful, highly advanced, intelligent, and complex in nature. They represent for us a real alternative to our own social environment.

And yet it isn't as though we have not had a hint of similar social structures in our recent history. The cult of the Goddess has existed in many historical cultures. She has taken the form of the goddesses Isis and Nut in Egypt, Demeter, Kore, and Hera in Greece, and more recently, as we have seen earlier, of the many apparitions of the Virgin Mary, which must surely represent a profound response to a deep and continuing awareness of the Mother Goddess.

Our awareness of these aspects of our heritage is not lacking, but the willingness to place them in positions of importance, high on our list of priorities, is.

We have been conditioned, and are still being conditioned by religious dogma, to believe that the power and authority of the male is more important than the female. Religion tells us that children are put on Earth by God, a male figure, and that the purpose of this is to provide fathers with, preferably, sons.

Children's surnames are derived from their fathers, the inheritance of land and goods traditionally passes from father to son. Succession to the English throne passes from the monarch first to the son. We are indoctrinated by such ideas on a daily basis, because at some time in history a tremendous force was put upon the human mind to get rid of any idea that raised women above the status of chattel. Past societies, and, we suggest, future societies, were, and could be again, very different.

In the Minoan civilization of ancient Crete, and those earlier societies that gave rise to it in Neolithic times, for a woman to be owned by a man, or even to take his name in marriage, would have seemed utterly strange.

As Nostradamus's verses gradually unfold their meaning, we begin to see that perhaps our future may be made up of a new understanding of what we have hitherto taken for granted, to our disadvantage.

Until recently we still chose to accept the misery of the man on the cross, rather than the joy of birth. But all that, according to Nostradamus, is about to change.

Women and God

There is little doubt that women in the twenty-first century are directly challenging the most sexist organizations in history—the institutions of religion.

Thousands of years of tradition, based on patriarchal values, have sustained the major religious institutions as exclusively male domains. In comparison with long past cultures such as the Neolithic, the Celtic, and others, this is a unique and very odd attitude to religion. What possible, real reasons could there be to exclude women, for example, from the priesthood? On the face of it, setting aside the traditional concepts, this exclusion seems to be an absurdity. And according to much that we can find in Nostradamus's verses, it will come rather smartly to an end in the twenty-first century.

> *Oh vast Rome, your ruin approaches,*
> *Not your walls, but your lifeblood and substance*
> *Someone with a sharp tongue will make a dent in*
>   *you,*
> *Harsh chains will be around it all.*
>   *—C10 V65[16]*

There are numerous verses such as this that can be interpreted to indicate the fall of the Church of Rome. It seems more likely, however, that the Catholic Church will not collapse completely, but will be transformed in some way; that the "lifeblood and substance" of this massive and outdated institution will find it necessary to change its structure to accommodate a changing world.

We can see something of the likely impression that women will make if we examine some of the changes that are currently taking place in the Church institutions of the world. For it won't simply be the Catholic Church that will face the demands of women, but all organized religious institutions, with a concomitant domino effect.

In November 1992, the General Synod of the Church of England voted to accept women into the priesthood.[17] This was probably one of the biggest victories enjoyed by women in centuries, and it had a major impact on the way women will be viewed in the future.

In American seminaries more than 34 percent of students are now women, and at Yale University School of Divinity half the students are women. At Harvard University's equivalent more than 60 percent of the students are women. These are incredible statistics, considering just how few women were involved in any aspect of organized religion just three decades ago—in fact, almost none.[18]

According to Patricia Aburdene and John Naisbitt in *Megatrends for Women*, there are now thousands of Catholic women worshipping in all-female groups today.[19] Nonorthodox Jewish women are embracing the traditional Orthodox mikveh bath as a spiritual and women's rights ritual.

And perhaps most dramatic of all, the American Episcopal Church elected its first woman bishop during the early 1990s.[20]

Aburdene reports that even the American Fundamentalist movement, probably the most intransigent religious movement outside the Catholic Church, is showing signs of change, as one of the most famous TV evangelists—Pat Robertson—started to work together with a woman—Sheila Walsh.[21]

Within Judaism, the Reform group has already proven to be the most flexible, with women now working as rabbis and cantors, and it will perhaps not be too long before the credo of the Orthodox is altered to accommodate new female attitudes and needs.

Perhaps this is the single most relevant aspect of what the feminine spirit will do for religion—that the ancient questions will be asked again. Why should we see God as either male or female? Was it really Jesus's intention that the Christian Church should develop into a male-dominated system? Where are women in the Bible? And why has Mary, the Mother of Christ, been represented as a symbol of passivity to fit in with the patriarchal view of women?

Questions such as these are being asked by women and form the basis of attitudes that will certainly transform the various Churches. The walls of Rome will perhaps not fall, but certainly the women's movement will alter the "lifeblood and substance" of Catholicism during the coming years.

Women and Power

> When Venus will be covered by the Sun
> Beneath the splendor will be a hidden form:
> Mercury will have exposed them to the fire,
> Through warlike noise it will be insulted.
> The Sun hidden eclipsed by Mercury,
> Will be placed only second in the sky:
> Of Vulcan Hermes she will make her pastures,
> The Sun will then be seen pure, glowing and golden
> —C4 V28–29[22]

The deciphering of Nostradamus's verses requires an understanding of the different metaphors employed. The Sun, in this and other verses, has been interpreted literally, as a metaphor for the New World and can also imply the dominant paradigm in power at any given moment, in this case men. In this verse we find the use of the Sun and Mercury both to describe the juxtaposition of man and woman and as an alchemical metaphor. The Sun, as man, has been in the ascendancy for many centuries, but now the complex and mercurial duality of man and woman together becomes the fashion for the future. In Roman mythology Mercury (in Greek, Hermes) is the messenger of the gods, symbol of communication and of duality—the double messages of rationality and irrationality. One of the biggest difficulties that men have faced in the past, and a reason perhaps why there is still often poor understanding between the sexes, is the apparent lack of "reason" behind feminine thought. Traditionally men have not been able to connect with feminine magic and the cyclical, often emotional changes that women undergo and have therefore chosen to suppress these human qualities in an attempt to remain ordered and consistent. But in these short lines Nostradamus can be interpreted as telling us that the mercurial elements of life will come into closer conjunction with the Sun, man, and take a stronger position in the affairs of everyday life.

We can also interpret the same lines through an alchemical metaphor, seeing the Sun as symbolizing gold or kind (matter which must die and be reborn). In this context, Nostradamus, who was well versed in alchemy, may be telling us that king/man must die and be reborn in harmony with the feminine spirit.

Essentially this verse prophecies that men will be eclipsed by women in the near future, and that even in matters of war, policing, and conflict, women will play a leading part. This is not to say, however, that the advent of feminine power will result in a continuation of the warfare that we have seen right through the twentieth century. There could be a very different scenario ahead of us.

During these days when women are still often forced to behave like men, we have seen a growth in the presence of women at war. There were 34–35,000 American women in active combat during the Gulf War.[23] During 1990 there were 227,018 women on active duty in the U.S. armed forces.[24] If we read the verse at the beginning of this chapter carefully, it appears that this increase in the number of women in the armed forces will somehow lead to a reduction in the instance of war. It will not be that armies will slowly become less male and more female, but that, perhaps, the presence of women in the arena of conflict will cause them to help us realize that war is a purposeless activity. Perhaps we can look at a free interpretation of this verse to find hints for the future.

At a time in the future when the love of woman will be overshadowed by men, beneath the bright shining light will be a hidden form. The mercurial nature of women will already have begun to expose men to a fiery new aspect of life, and through militancy on the part of women this maleness will be exposed and insulted. Man will eventually become hidden in his turn by woman, and will be placed only second in importance. Using her newfound power she will make new pastures, and men will find a new respect in life that will make them shine again in a better light.

When Nostradamus writes about men shading a hidden form in women, we can read into this, perhaps, more than the obvious.

Let us take a look at a theory currently being examined by science.

The scientists Francisco Varela and Humberto Maturana in South America have studied what they call the "autoposis" of living systems.[25] Their work may be seen to be based on a hypothesis that has long been examined and understood from a less scientific viewpoint in Eastern religions such as Hinduism and some of the modern religious teachings of, for example, J. Krishnamurti and Osho Rajneesh.[26] This is that the mind operates rather like an elaborate tape-recording machine, absorbing information and recording the results, and then acts upon those results on a perpetual, habitual level thereafter. According to this view, rather than being the masterly and vital entity upon which the Western world has based most of understanding, the mind is little more, at least in this context, than a parrot, capable only of reiteration and lacking any originality.

Systems that are learned or imprinted upon the mind—systems such as those engendered by patriarchal society—are maintained in the human mind through a process that could be called replication. This replication, or self-copying ability, occurs within the actual DNA code, affecting the individual at all levels of conscious and unconscious awareness—in the very cells of the body, within the psychology of individuals, and thereby into the social environment they occupy. This replication of ideas, which may not always result in the best for the individual or society, is the very basis for the maintenance of any social structure, good or bad. In a sense, we are all rather like parrots in a jungle that has been constructed by us, for our benefit or disadvantage, without the true wisdom.

The biologist Rupert Sheldrake has developed a scientific (though in the current climate still regarded as renegade) theory of what he terms "morphic resonance," which describes this concept of replication in a similar way. He maintains that we are surrounded by, and contained within, habit fields that keep all the habitual functions of nature and life going simply because they have always done so. He says that a new habit—such as, for example, when the first aspirin crystals were formed—is more difficult to formulate because there is no existing morphic field to give it shape. But once the formulation is made, and repeated, it becomes easier and easier. We can see our patriarchal morphic fields in this light. Patriarchy has been learned over a long period of time, and therefore everything within this morphic resonance is continuously repeating itself, no matter whether it is right for the occupants of the field or not.[27]

The replicated information that leads to a patriarchal culture would not work for a culture based on partnership, for example. Patriarchal replicate thought patterns are founded on domination, aggression, and fear, while the thoughts replicated for the creation of a partnership culture are based on equality, receptiveness, mutual concern, and love. What two formats could be further apart than these? And yet, what can be perceived from reading Nostradamus's verses is that we may be in transit from one to the other right at this moment.

The hidden form referred to in the verse is, according to this interpretation, the replicate code needed to alter society from a dominant, patriarchal mode to a partnership mode, and women are the holders of the key.

But how, we may ask, could such a change occur? Given

that every single human mind would have to change in order for the new replication to have any effect, how and from what source can this transformation come about?

The simple answer lies in the fact that it has already happened before. In order for the present situation to come about, a massive new replication took place in our history, a re-replication that resulted in the transformation from a partnership culture to the present patriarchal model.

It happened, if you like, in reverse. Now we hope to reverse it again, and return to a world where the values can improve.

During the evolution of monotheism by the early Hebrews, the Christians, and then the Muslims, there was massive destruction of the old partnerships created by thousands of years of pagan values. Ancient temples were destroyed, sacred Celtic tree groves cut down, people slaughtered, wars fought, witches burned, and thousands of individuals persecuted, all in the name of a new replication of ideas that civilization believed to be the best. "Convert or die" was the theme of the Church, as we have already seen in this book.

And this has had an incredibly powerful and long-lasting effect on the individual persona—on the mind, habits, beliefs, and fears of each of us. We still cross ourselves against evil, without asking why a cross, and what is evil anyway? We still believe in a devil and a god as opposites. We seldom stop to ask what the source of these two entities might be, or whether they are connected. The questions have been asked:

Who made the world?

Why, God, of course.

And who created sin?

Why, the devil, of course.

And who made the devil?

Why, God, of course.

So who then is the ultimate sinner?

These connections were lost somewhere down the ages, recorded as they were in *grimoires*—books of spells—suppressed by the "word of God," now repeated by us, often parrot fashion.[28]

So, what we may read into the lines of Nostradamus's verses is that woman rises out of the shadow and begins to help us create a new replicate code—a long, perhaps arduous, process but one that will contribute to the single biggest cultural evolutionary change to occur for over two thousand years.

Interestingly enough, a fundamental reason for the writing of this book was the realization that ancient conditioning had caused most interpreters of Nostradamus's verses to base their predictions largely on factors—such as war, conflict, fear, and disaster—that are entirely familiar to a patriarchal society. Whereas if we don the cap of an alternative, and still entirely possible, cultural system, many of the verses read totally differently. We see largely through the eyes of our beliefs, and only with some determination can we begin to discern shadows that may be hidden by the overwhelming light of preexisting conditioning—the current dominant replication.

We read on in this verse that:

*The mercurial nature of women will already have
begun to expose men to a fiery new aspect of life,
and through militancy on the part of women this
maleness will be exposed and insulted.*

This echo of the earlier verses relating to the march of the
Seline Movement across Europe—the militancy on the part of
women—helps portray the more mercurial aspect of the feminine spirit, a characteristic that many of us, both male and
female, will welcome, but many may not!

*Man will eventually become hidden in his turn by
woman, and will be placed only second in importance.
Using her newfound power she will make new
pastures, and men will find a new respect in life that
will make them shine again in a better light.*

But everything that goes around comes around again, and
men, though hidden in their turn by the much-increased
strength of the female spirit, will come back into their own in
a more equal and balanced manner and thereby find greater
respect for life. Perhaps this will be the decisive change,
which will contribute in turn to an improvement in the present
levels of global pollution—the result of a respect for birth and
life rather than suffering and death. In order for this to happen, it is likely that the groundswell of new female voters will
influence the political power positions of the world—most
likely in the form of a female American president.

The First Female President of the United States

The Moon in the full of night over the high
*   mountain,*
The new wise one with a lone brain seen there:
By her disciples invited to be immortal,
Eyes at noon. Hands on bosoms, bodies in the fire.
            —C4 V31[29]

This slightly obscure verse begins our hunt for a female president of the United States. Perhaps the most important single clue in the verse lies in the original French version, which employs the word *sophe* in the second line—*Le nouveau sophe d'un seul cerveau la vu.* The word derives from both Greek and Latin—*sophos*—and means "wise one." On a simple level Nostradamus could plainly have been indicating the presence of a wise individual with a good brain (*cerveau*), which stands alone (*seul*). She is, according to the third line, invited by her disciples, or supporters, to become immortal. She is seen (or is watching) either at noon or to the south, her hands on her bosom and her body in the fire. What can all this mean?

The first words in this line in the French version read *Yeux au midi.* This can mean either: "eyes of midday" or "eyes to the south." If we accept the version that tells us "eyes to the south," we might suppose that this individual, a woman, who will be made immortal by her followers, will come from the south of the United States.

On the day that all this comes to fruition, the moon is full and seen over a high mountain.

Given these general observations and the specific hints in

the quatrain, the suggestion is that Nostradamus's verse is guiding us toward a location for the first female president in the southern regions of the United States. There are, of course, from a political point of view, a number of candidates for this position, and we can only conjecture as to who might get the job. Who can resist speculating on who will become the first woman president? Will she be a Republican or a Democrat? Will she ascend to the presidency after serving as a vice president? Many would welcome Governor Ann Richards' wit and outstanding speaking ability on the presidential campaign trail. In that department, she is certainly superior to every presidential candidate in recent history.

Additional detail may help to give shape to the prediction. Perhaps the final celebrations for a female president will be held near a mountain or high hill at night at a full moon. Perhaps, in her elation at the result, she will place her hands across her bosom (in any event this is probably allegorical). For certain, the first woman to become president of the United States will be "in the fire" of political conflict from the very moment she steps into her new position. And there are other prophecies in Nostradamus's writings that strengthen this interpretation. The above is, of course, largely conjecture, as Nostradamus's prophetic vision is, as ever, vague and convoluted. There is no certainty, of course, that this first female president will be a successful one, and in fact there are a number of verses in the *Centuries* that indicate that she will have many problems and perhaps end up something of a failure.

When the eclipse of the Sun will have occurred,
The monster will be seen in the fullness of the day:

In quite another way will it be interpreted,
A high price unguarded and none will have
     foreseen it.

                              —C3 V34[30]

This verse gives us the impression that once woman has managed to take a more powerful and more equal role in government (after the Sun, man, is eclipsed), once she is seen in the full light of day, she turns out, perhaps, whoever she may be in this particular case, to be a monster! And in the passion of the feminist movement, no one would have predicted that the first woman to succeed to power would end up not succeeding in power.

The Secret Society of Women

By means of the supreme power of eternal God, we
     are led by the Moon:
Before she has completed her entire cycle, the Sun
     will come and then Saturn. For according to the
     signs of the heavens, the reign of Saturn will
     return; so that all told, the world is drawing
     near to an anaragonic revolution.

                         —Preface to his
                          son César[31]

Throughout the recent history of the West there have been many secret societies. We have seen the Gnostics, the Knights Templar, the Rosicrucians, and many others, including even heretical messianic sects within Judaism, which have been forced by necessity to remain in the protection of the shadows because of persecution by other belief systems. These secret "societies" concealed themselves from the repression of moralistic attitudes that they could not support, but also could not stand up against. In order to sustain their own credos and beliefs, they often built whole social structures in secret, with rules and laws devised to govern the embattled few who were sustained by the knowledge of compatriotism and the drama and tension of secrecy. For some years in America similar structures were created by repressed minorities, such as black people and, subsequently, the gay community.

Wherever a particular unit is under fire from the larger society, it will tend to gather in groups to find mutual support. Society as a whole is essentially like a giant, and often monstrous, animal. It will support only those that adhere to its rules. Religious cults down the ages (including Christianity) have suffered at the hands of this monster, and only by enough determination, energy, and force have minority groups surfaced to find a place in, and so alter, the society they initially disrupted.

Earlier we discussed the verses prophesying a movement of women that would result in a mass march across parts of Europe and called it the Seline Movement.

The quatrains give a strong sense of a band of women who have gathered together to make the march occur. This band is seeking not simply equal rights in a male-dominated society, but complete freedom to function in all respects on equal terms with men. This is yet to come.

Nostradamus's words give a definite sense of conspiracy—the badly conceived secret is mentioned—and there is a feeling of common purpose, as the gathering of women determines to make an impact on the society that has suppressed them for so many centuries. In essence, events, such as the Seline March, and the election of the first American female president, are leading up to the emergence of women into society, out of secrecy. In the last decades of the twentieth century women, in effect, had to create a secret society among themselves and only in the latter years of that century and the early years of this one will they come completely out of the closet, so to speak.

This interpretation of *Century* 2:73–82 is reinforced by another part of Nostradamus's prophetic work—a letter to his son César, a few lines of which are set out at the head of this section. Let us consider these step by step.

> *By means of the supreme power of eternal God, we*
> *are led by the Moon.*

Nostradamus makes references to the Moon throughout his prophecies, and although this occasionally refers to the Moon itself, there are far more instances of the use of the Moon as a metaphor for the state of womankind. Lunar cycles are too short to be used as an astrological directive for timing the prophecies, so we can assume that in this case, Nostradamus is referring to the Moon metaphorically. Thus, we are led by woman. This may be so in any event, but it is particularly so in relation to a future where the feminine spirit has grown in strength in the world.

> *. . . before she has completed her entire cycle, the Sun*
> *will come and then Saturn.*

Nostradamus tells us that the newfound power of women will be rising, that it will not have completed its full cycle of transformation, when men (the Sun) return to a position of equality once again.

For many men during the late twentieth century, feminism posed problems, in the sense that they have frequently felt diminished by the crimes and mistakes that their past has imposed upon them. The male of our species has been forced to reexamine his sexuality, his power, his ego, and many, if not most, of his previously established attitudes. As feminism takes a stronger hold in the worlds of politics, the Church, and business, so the disenfranchisement of the male will be felt still more. But eventually the pendulum will swing back and men will begin to understand that there is a place in the world for them beside women rather than above them, as they imagined themselves to be in the past. New attitudes for women will produce new attitudes for men.

Finally in this line we are told that Saturn will return also. This is a fascinating piece of metaphorical description, for in astrological interpretation Saturn is generally associated with the male planets. But this has arisen only because the patriarchal attitude of the interpreters has dictated it. True, in Greek mythology the Titan Cronus (in Latin, Saturn) castrated his father Uranus and swallowed his own children (so becoming identified with Time, the devourer of all things). However, in a war with the gods led by Zeus, he was defeated and withdrew with the Titans to found a kingdom in the farthest west. Thus, the power associated with the planet Saturn was, in ancient Greece, that of peace. Saturn has an earth energy, and earth energies are almost always feminine. Astrologically Saturn rules Capricorn, a feminine, earth sign, and Saturn is also concerned (among other things) with conservation and maintenance—again, feminine characteristics. What Nostradamus indicates here is the return of harmony after conflict.

For anyone who knows a little about modern astrology, one of the most troublesome and complex periods of any young individual's life is the point at which Saturn returns. Put another way—when we are born, Saturn is in a particular part of the astrological environment, and on its recurring course through the heavens and through our lives, this exact position occurs on the next full orbit around Earth. This takes approximately twenty-eight years. The period of the Saturn return can often be a traumatic one for an individual, and at around twenty-eight years of age, when we reach the beginning of the fifth seven-year cycle, we often reach a stage in our lives where dramatic, sometimes painful change occurs. This Saturn return is seen in astrology as an event that stands apart from the characteristics of the planet Saturn, and therefore we can accept perhaps that Nostradamus was giving us a series of metaphors and warnings within the one reference to the planet.

We can deduce, therefore, that Nostradamus may be telling us that the Saturn return of the feminist movement will occur once men have come back to some form of equality, after the women's movement has made its mark. At this point women will encounter problems with their newfound positions in life and in the new society they have helped to create. If we suppose that the real women's movement began in the early 1990s, we can project this prophecy as taking effect toward the end of the second decade of this millennium. The last line in this piece then adds a strange, enigmatic finale:

For according to the signs of the heavens, the reign of Saturn will return; so that all told, the world is drawing near to an anaragonic revolution.

The word "anaragonic" has troubled interpreters of Nostradamus's prophecies from the very beginning. Edgar Leoni, perhaps the most thorough of the recent interpreters, suggests that La Pelletier's earlier interpretation may be correct and that the word derives from the Geek words *anairesin-gonichos*, which mean "destruction-engendering."[32] This idea, given that it bears only a remote and somewhat tortuous resemblance to the pseudo-French word in Nostradamus's text, probably mostly derives from the war-conscious mind of the twenty-first century.

Another interpretation comes from Fortune Rigaud, who suggests that the word grew out of either the Greek word *anaxagora*, which means a sovereign mob, or *Anaxagoras*, the name of the Greek philosopher and tutor of Pericles, who predicted the end of the world through fire and water. Nostradamus, however, would not have intended such a description to be taken at face value.

As discussed in another book by the author, *Nostradamus: The Millennium and Beyond*, end-of-the-world scenarios are a subject of great interest, possibly because they become a macrocosmic version of the individual human fear of death.[33] We project our personal fears upon the world. We expect that the world will end in some shattering and apocalyptic cataclysm, probably brought about either by the pressing of a certain "red button" by a foolish politician or as a result of the wanton neglect of our environment. We suppose that we have sufficient power to overcome the natural power of the cosmos, and that our dream of disaster will be greater than the dream the cosmos has of itself. And this tendency reaches a peak around the turn of a millennium.

The most likely solution can be found when we consider Nostradamus's own time. The Greek prefix *an-* means "not" or "without."[34] Thus, *anaragonique* means "not Aragonic." What, then, was the "Aragonic" revolution?

When Ferdinand II of Aragon married Isabella I of Castile in 1469, so uniting the two kingdoms, Spain became one of the greatest powers in the world. Having expelled the Moors and Jews in the name of religious and racial purity, and established the infamous Spanish Inquisition, they were granted the title of *los reyes católicos*, "the Catholic kings." Under their successors, Charles I and Philip II, the Spanish maritime empire controlled Central and South America, Naples, Sicily, Milan, and the Netherlands and posed a permanent threat to France. Such a rapid rise in fortunes and shift of power must have seemed to Spain's neighbors nothing less than revolutionary. Conquering in the name of God, the most aggressively patriarchal power in Europe seemed to be reaping the rewards of greed, intolerance, and military might.

Nostradamus was wise enough to see beyond this. The "unaragonic revolution" he was referring to embodies the opposite attributes. It is that peaceful revolution that will occur when the feminine spirit finally triumphs over the masculine and gives humanity its first real glimpse of wisdom, a wisdom that it has profoundly lacked until now.

This revolution will certainly mean the end of the world as we know it, though this may not be apparent to all of us. But those who are watching the way the world evolves will undoubtedly notice, for this could be the single biggest revolution the world has ever known. It will arise from the Secret Society of Women, which already exists. Unlike male secret societies, however, the female version needs no written constitution, no fixed rules, and no central government, for the Secret Society of Women is an unspoken, mutable bond that could not be sustained by the male spirit. It has no boundaries and thereby makes no wars.

Feminine Magic

A growing feature of the latter years of the twentieth century was the apparent increase in the occurrence of unexplained phenomena. There were more reported sightings of UFOs, more ghost hunts, more bizarre, often apparently impossible happenings in those years than in the previous hundred. There are corn circles, extraordinary and precise earth markings in Europe and the United States, which, despite the attempts of rationalists and skeptics, still defy real explanation. There are literally thousands of reports of UFO sightings and alien encounters, numerous ghostly apparitions, and reports of events that cannot be explained within normal parameters.

What is perhaps not understood by those who seek to discount such phenomena is the revived human need to believe in magic. The scientific age and the modern passion for the deification of the mind have temporarily spoiled our belief in the irrational, the instinctual, the magical, and the inexplicable. Our fundamental, renewed interest in such things is an expression of the irrepressible human love of mystery.

The return, once again, of women to center stage will bring back that lost magic and help create a world where logic and rationality are subsumed by beauty, taste, and magic spells!

Magical capability is predominantly a female quality, though this does not mean that men do not possess it in some measure. Sadly, the overimportance of science, technology, and the pressures of a competitive, aggressive world seem to reduce the instinctual capacity in men; so there has been a tendency in the past, and there still is in the present, though perhaps less so, for those in command to suppress these so-called "useless" qualities in women.

But Nostradamus has something to say about this too.

> *The lover's heart is opened by furtive love*
> *The woman ravished by floods of tears:*
> *The lascivious will mimic*
> *With moral indignation,*
> *The father will twice do without the soul.*
> *—C8 V25[35]*

This verse is a classic among Nostradamus's quatrains, for it leaves almost all interpreters completely at a loss. First, it doesn't fit with the "warring" viewpoint of our twenty-first-century fears. Nobody seems to be dying, and no battles are being fought. There is no end-of-the-world scenario and no society in the midst of a catastrophic plague. And second, it is difficult to interpret from within a patriarchal conditioning, being about love, sex, and the soul.

These subjects may well acquire the greatest significance of all once the feminine perspective prevails. Men have not, generally speaking, paid a great deal of attention to love or the soul as issues in the past. They have paid attention to sex, but in a way that has caused much heartache, largely through the suppression of the natural sexuality that is available within the human psyche, or put another way, the male-dominated societies have chosen to suppress female sexuality. Patriarchal society has attempted to reduce our openness, to fetter our free sexual spirits with shameful, furtive attitudes, starting from the very earliest age. Education has taken the form of heavily conditioned, often pornographic (sex without love) messages. American society as a whole displays a strange imbalance of sexual display and repression, with every newsstand and cinema offering an unlimited range of the weirdest, most revolting, and "kinky" sexuality to the public, while at the same time the "normal" attitude toward sex is very much "under the counter," preferring to sneer at human intimacy.

This distorted approach to sexuality and love is derived from a deeply ingrained conditioning, largely brought about by organized religious dogma, which has attached sex to sin, as though the most fundamental activity of human nature were somehow bad!

It is not that we truly believe it to be bad when we consider it soberly, but our unconscious attitudes are so deeply ingrained that we habitually react as though we think it bad.

This unconscious attitude is transmitted to our offspring equally unconsciously. It is not that we really mean to pass on such nonsense, but without realizing it parents will avoid direct explanation of sexual behavior (particularly their own, about which they are invariably embarrassed) because they don't understand how it works themselves, so they inevitably educate their children in the light of this poor knowledge.

Sexual education within our school systems, even in the last years of the twenty-first century, still carries a strong element of guilt and so creates a confusion among pupils, and the pupils themselves often educate one another in ways that are so confused, unhappy, and furtive that the result can take years to put right and may never be completely cleared out of the adult psyche.

And what is worst of all about this cycle of behavior is the fact that sex is connected with the emotions. It is connected with love and the soul, and if the basic understanding of sexuality is besmirched by foolish education, the individual becomes unable to love effectively, unable to express emotions properly and freely, and therefore unable to grasp the inspiration that is available from the soul itself. There is, in effect, a battlement built up around the individual psyche that will neither let anything fresh and innocent in nor allow true emanations of feelings and moods out.

What we have in the verse at the beginning of this section is a direct reference to the effects of the death of patriarchy. Let us take the lines more freely:

> *The heart is opened because of a furtive love, and by the fact that women have so long been ravished by floods of tears. The lascivious of the past will parody this development with moral indignation, and the patriarchal world will realize that it has so long done without the soul.*

Having tired of sexual repression, our true sexuality will eventually be liberated by the greater presence of the feminine spirit. Hypocrites who continue to pretend moral indignation because of religious attitudes or false social controls will sneer still, because however free a society may be, there will always be the negative and foolish element somewhere. But most important of all, in the last line, patriarchal attitudes (the father in the original verse) will yield gladly once women demonstrate the true value of natural and free sexuality, which gives access to the soul, to inspiration, and most of all to love—which, however clichéd it may sound, is the only cure.

Transforming the World

Before long all will be rearranged,
We can hope for a very sinister century,
The estate that was masked and alone will change,
Few will wish to stay as they were.
                              —C2 V10[36]

We have seen in earlier chapters some of the ways in which women will move in large numbers into higher and more influential positions in society—in politics, the priesthood, and business—while maintaining their essential difference from the patriarchal past.

Our society remains, at the beginning of the twenty-first century, very much a society of men. Attitudes are still almost completely patriarchal, for patriarchy as a system has been around too long to be disposed of or transformed quickly. The whole preoccupation with war, with armies, for example, is based on a patriarchal, protective concept that somehow we need either fight with or defend against one another in order to live safely.

Nations are ruled by men's ideas, ideas of aggression, domination, fear. We have been told that such ideas are not the only models for effective rules and order. In fact, the ideas themselves are what help to perpetuate the aggression, domination, and fear. There are other ways, but we have lived in patriarchies for so long that we have forgotten the alternatives. According to Nostradamus, and other prophets, our present social structures will fall by the wayside as women bring a greater influence to the world in numbers and in determination. A critical mass is needed for this to occur.

The process will still take time and struggle, though in this age of rapid change it will not be so long that most of us will not live to see the prophecy at the beginning of this chapter fulfilled.

Having seen something of the ways in which women will acquire greater influence, we are now able to look at the changes that will occur as a result of that influence. Nostradamus has helped us to envisage a fresh paradigm, a nonpatriarchal society on Earth for the first time in thousands of years.

Opening the Doors to the Feminine

First perhaps we can try to see what might emerge from a critical mass of the feminine spirit. Where and how would such a transformation of energy impact on our world? What feminine characteristics would we find predominant after this change?

In order to identify potential characteristics of the emergent femininity, we will take note of some of the best feminist writing of the last few years. Once we have made a brief "list," we will seek advice from Nostradamus, by looking at relevant verses from his *Centuries*.

> *We are all familiar with legends about an earlier,*
> *more harmonious and peaceful age. The Bible tells of*
> *a garden where woman and man lived in harmony*
> *with each other and nature—before a male god*
> *decreed that woman henceforth be subservient to*
> *man. The Chinese Tao Te Ching describes a time*
> *when the yin, or feminine principle, was not yet*
> *ruled by the male principle, the yang, a time when*
> *the wisdom of the mother was still honored and*
> *followed above all.*
> —*Riane Eisler,* The Chalice and the Blade[37]

Harmony, then, may be considered a potential characteristic of this new society.

Harmony arises out of balance and acceptance and out of learning to put aspects of human nature, such as domination, competitive anxiety, and mutual concern, in their proper places.

This is not to say that the competitive spirit will disappear or that individuals will not continue to be dominating or anxious, but these characteristics may be seen as existing in minority situations, not predominating in government, Church, and State as they do today.

Nostradamus tells us that *few will wish to stay as they were.* While we may look forward to a new world in which the change is for the better, some may cling to the familiar life of misery that has been engendered by patriarchy. After all, we can grow attached to our neuroses.

> *In every dimension of life there is a sense of old molds cracked or cracking, of the precious—or rancid—contents spilling out, but there is no vision of a human future . . . Humans have reached a stage from which it is almost impossible to imagine a future . . . we are utterly bankrupt of vision. And the barrenness of our imagination, our hope and faith, could result in the annihilation of our race. This book rests on the assumptions that our present lack of vision as well as the present condition of the world is the result of the failure of our morality; that it is possible for humans to create and live by a different morality; and that only by adopting a new morality can we restore enough emotional, physical and intellectual equilibrium to create a more felicitous society.*
> —*Marilyn French*, Beyond Power[38]

Second, then, in our list of important characteristics of the feminine new world is a *new morality.* The first line of the quatrain at the beginning of this chapter tells us that *before long all will be rearranged.* One of those rearrangements will have to be a new morality, and that morality perhaps will come from a completely new viewpoint, provided by the acceptance and acknowledgment of the ancient ways that grew out of respect for the Mother Goddess.

> *As women and men re-sort out the issues that have divided them, and seek a deeper, more creative level of partnership, men will want and need to know about the trends shaping women's lives, about the new activities women engage in.*
> —Patricia Aburdene and John Naisbitt,
> Megatrends for Women[39]

Third comes *cooperation* between men and women and a genuine desire in men to know what women are about and what they need in life. This attitude has been singularly lacking in the past, and only very recently have men begun to give up belittling the efforts of women because of their fear of inferiority. Fear of inferiority and the compulsion to belittle arise out of a need to control, and cooperation requires no control. It either comes naturally or it doesn't exist. Most of the wars that are still being fought around the world arise out of the absurd notion that land can be owned by people, that a country should have more land under its control than it already has. This concept was given birth on the day men decided to parcel up territory for the benefit of their sons. Cooperation would ameliorate and monitor this possessive tendency in different ways, perhaps by opening up borders, as has occurred, for example, in Europe. And on the more practical side:

> *Women lack a positive emotional vocabulary about money. While many great stories about men are*

stories about the romance between men and riches,
women have very little narrative relationship to the
idea of wealth, or the drama of seeking, building or
losing a fortune.

—*Naomi Wolf,* Fire with Fire[40]

Nostradamus, in the verse at the top of this chapter, tells us that *the estate that was masked and alone will change*, and one of the ways that it will have to change is toward a much greater degree of involvement by women in the global economy, for essentially men have made a terrible mess of this vital aspect of human affairs. Before the genderquake reaches a stage of cooperation and harmony it will need to go through a period of *discovery*, specifically in relation to financial and political behavior. It may not be enough for women to equal men in their knowledge of economics, for this would only mean a continuation of financial inequality around the world, a continuation of starvation, poverty for the majority, and vast, unnecessary wealth in the hands of a tiny minority.

One of the characteristics that will enhance this new feminine world will therefore be a willingness to discover and thereby *innovate*.

Adam Maxwell, age twenty-four, husband to Ruth. A
boy who wants to go to the top. As if the world has a
top!

—*Octavia Waldo,* Roman Spring[41]

Contrary to popular conceptions, probably the greatest contribution of the feminine paradigm in the future will be its *spirituality*. Women will help men to understand that their ambitions are not the be-all and end-all of life. And for men, this will begin by being a "very sinister" change, for men take their ambitions very seriously indeed. This is not to say that women don't also take ambition seriously, because they are still strongly influenced by patriarchy. Once the critical mass is reached, many of these things will change.

So we are looking, perhaps, for a world that will eventually, because of the feminine spirit, reach a new estate—one that contains harmony, in at least a greater measure than today, and coperation between nations, people, and races. It will also develop new ways of looking at the fundamental aspects of industry and economics, such as the way money is related to human effort. And finally, women will bring a new spirituality and maturity to society, helping men to learn the truth about ambition, domination, and competition, and so avoid replicating all the same habits, generation after generation.

The Great Dame Is Born

One of Nostradamus's most dramatic series of prophecies occurs in an "Epistle" he wrote to Henry II, the King of France, during the latter part of his life. This remarkable document literally outlines the future history of the world. In many parts it is so accurate that it leaves the reader astonished, because Nostradamus set out the future in a way that no other prophet had ever done or has done since.

Some pages into the very long letter, there are a few lines that concern our subject, and they read as follows:

For God will pay attention to the long barrenness of the great dame, who will conceive two principal children. But she will be at risk, and the female she will give birth to will also, because of the fears of the age, be at risk of death by the age of eighteen years, and will not survive beyond thirty-six years. She will leave three males, and one female, and of these two will not have had the same father.

There will be great differences between the three brothers, and then there will be great co-operation and agreement between them that three and four parts of Europe will be disrupted. The youngest one will help to sustain the Christian Church and beneath him new sects will be elevated and then will fall, Arabs will be driven away, kingdoms united and new laws made.

—The Epistle to Henry II[42]

The debate surrounding these words, and those in the rest of the Epistle to Henry II, has continued since Nostradamus was first interpreted. Is the "Great Dame" related to France? Or is she related to communism, or fascism, or Europe, or the French Queen, Catherine de' Medici? Are the two principal children chosen from among Catherine's seven surviving offspring—could they be Francis II, perhaps, and Elizabeth, who married Philip II of Spain? Who will this child be who sustains the Christian Church, and what will the sects be that come and go beneath him?

None of these questions has ever been answered effectively. There have not been, since Nostradamus's time, any kings who fit the above description. Nor have there been any events that accord with the passage.

Of course, we could say that Nostradamus simply got it wrong, and leave it there. But so much of the rest of the Epistle has proved accurate that we may presume that if this part of it has not been borne out by events, it is simply because they have not yet occurred.

It is the author's contention that these lines apply to events, specific in nature, in our future, and that they relate to the major influence of feminism, partly forming an allegory of what we will see happen during the early years of the twenty-first century and partly relating specifically to individuals in our future.

The prophecy begins with an allegory with a clear meaning—that the *great dame*, which we can easily interpret as woman, will *conceive two principal children*. Nostradamus does not say "give birth to" two children.

The French word *concevoir* can also mean "to design," so it is entirely possible that Nostradamus was telling us of a grand design by woman to create two new principles.

> *God will pay attention to the long barrenness of*
> *   woman,*
> *Who will design two new principles.*

Next we read that this "barren woman," the allegorical feminine spirit that has so long been neglected by the world (and certainly by God), although she will have conceived these two principles, will soon be in danger—some eighteen years after the principles have been conceived.

> *But she will be at risk, and the female she will give*
> *birth to will also, because of the fears of the age, be*
> *at risk of death by the age of eighteen years, and will*
> *not survive beyond thirty-six years.*

And these principles will not work beyond thirty-six years. If we go back to our established time line—where we decided that the beginning of the real feminist movement occurred in the early 1990s—then the women's movement will, by this interpretation, start to show cracks around the year 2008 and by 2026 will have failed, at least in terms of the principles that were conceived in the early years.

But it is also suggested that Nostradamus was not merely giving us an allegorical statement, but linking it to actual individuals in our future. The logic behind this is derived from the fact that we are given a kind of lineage in the lines that follow.

> *She will leave three males, and one female, and of*
> *these, two will not have had the same father.*

We mentioned the date 2008 as being the beginning of some sort of downfall, or further transformation, of the feminist movement. This year happens to be the end of the second term of our proposed first woman president of the United States, who we have suggested might be Ann Richards, the former governor of Texas, or Barbara Box, California senator. It is also worth noting that if we take Nostradamus's information literally, then the first woman president of the United States should have four children, *three males, and one female.* Ann Richards has four children, Cecile, Daniel, Clarke, and Ellen— two boys and two girls—perhaps close enough! It is not suggested that two of them had different fathers, but they might each have followed a different spiritual mentor.

> *There will be great differences between the three brothers, and then there will be great co-operation and agreement between them that three and four parts of Europe will be disrupted. The youngest one will help to sustain the Christian Church and beneath him new sects will be elevated and then will fall, Arabs will be driven away, kingdoms united and new laws made.*

There are similarities between this prophetic Epistle and the verses that we examined earlier surrounding the Seline Movement and the march across Europe. In that series we found mention of three wreaths and three sisters, which were also interpreted allegorically as relating to the banner of the Seline Movement and the principles of femininity.

In this case we read of three sons and a daughter being born out of the established women's movement or an individual within it, and further hints inform us that there will be great *cooperation* between these three sons, so that much of Europe will be affected. Could these children be the offspring of a prominent female figure in world politics? Could they in fact become famous individuals, who will work in politics in the coming years, following in the footsteps of their mother? This would already be a major step for the feminine revolution, for in the past, patriarchal society has dictated the pattern "like father, like son." Perhaps now we may coin a new cliché—"like mother, like child." In any event, if we are to believe in this prophecy, and if it is more than coincidence that our first female president of the United States, if we have the correct name, has four children, then perhaps those four children will be instrumental in the affairs of Europe and of the Christian Church during the first few decades of the twenty-first century.

Female Lines

After prophesying the presence of a great dame who gives birth to four children, the Epistle to Henry II continues on the same theme. It seems, if we interpret the words correctly, that the children of the first woman president of the United States are active in a number of important national and international arenas during the first decades of the twenty-first century. It can also be shown that their positions in the political and religious worlds of the United States and Europe enable them to further the progress of feminine power in the future. We will examine each set of lines in turn.

> *The oldest child will be involved with the country*
> *whose banner shows angry crowned lions with paws*
> *resting on intrepid arms. The second child in age*
> *will run far, in accompaniment with Latin people,*
> *until a second and furious path is taken to Mount*
> *Louis. From here he will go down to then cross the*
> *Pyrenees which will not become owned by the*

ancient power. The third child will cause great
human suffering, and for a long time the month of
March will not be a religious period.
          —The Epistle to Henry II[43]

The eldest child will, within this interpretation, become involved in Scotland. The arms of Scotland at the time when Nostradamus was alive bore a crowned lion sitting on a crowned helmet with a sword in its paw. (An alternative theory is that she will be active in the province of Nova Scotia, in southeastern Canada—the St. Lawrence river had been explored by Cartier for France in 1534.)

The second child also looks like he will have a fairly exciting and far-reaching future, connected with a "Latin" country. In Nostradamus's terms this would be either a Latin America country or Italy. And as the next reference takes our intrepid second child to Mount Louis we can be fairly sure that Nostradamus was talking about Italy. Mount Louis can be fairly reliably identified as the Great St. Bernard Pass—Mount Louis (the original old French description in Nostradamus's book) refers to the Latin *Mons Jovis*, which in turn refers to the St. Bernard Pass over the Swiss Alps. From here, he will evidently travel from Switzerland through France and across the Pyrenees into the Iberian Peninsula. This area will *not become owned by the ancient power.* Could this refer to a newly independent Basque country, or Catalonia, pointing to a new regional European confederation?

The third child of the future female president, according to our frame of reference, is associated with some adverse influence in the world, which causes suffering in an area connected with religion.

Finally, we hear about the fourth member of the family.

> *The daughter will become involved with the*
> *preservation of the Christian Church. Her husband*
> *will fall into contact with religious sects and of her*
> *two children, one will remain faithful to the*
> *Catholic Church and the other will become involved*
> *with a sect.*
>
> —The Epistle to Henry II[44]

Following our logic, it seems that the youngest member of the new president's family will have some influence on the Church. In this case Nostradamus would have been referring to the Catholic Church. We could interpret this quite easily as meaning that this child will perhaps become one of the first female Catholic priests. Nostradamus even goes on to predict that the new president's children will also have religious affiliations, one to the same Church and the other with what he refers to as a "pagan" sect.

All this might sound somewhat bizarre—it seems unreal to make interpretations such as these about individuals we know little about, people who have not yet achieved fame or impinged upon global consciousness. However, if and when these individuals rise above the "water," so to speak, it will seem totally natural that they should figure in the realm of global affairs.

We have, up to now, interpreted these enigmatic lines in a fairly literal fashion, but if we accept the idea of a feminine influence in the future, a fairly secure assumption, then what we could be looking at is a broader and perhaps more allegorical meaning. The essence of what Nostradamus is telling us, if we take this seriously, is that there will be a strong alliance between America and Europe that will occur as a result of the presence of a female president.

The United States of Europe

Given that the European community has begun the process of attempting to create firm alliances between fourteen nations in the same region, and that this grouping will almost certainly be extended to include a number of other countries—perhaps including the Eastern European and the Baltic nations—it seems likely that this greatly more powerful "nation" of nations will become as powerful as the United States of America.

Given also that we are discussing the rise of the feminine spirit in the future, the ethos of *cooperation* may eventually replace the drive for empowerment or domination. "Superna-tions" may perhaps not be so concerned to dominate. They may actually become intelligent for the first time in their long careers and seek *harmony*. In this case there will be an interim period, while the new paradigm accesses its result, a period when the United States and Europe are courting one another for alliance.

It could be interpreted, therefore, that the new American female president will have a big part to play in this accessing of alliances. Nostradamus may be telling us that we can expect a more formal connection to occur between the United States of America and the European Community, which will result in a superpower to beat all superpowers, but in the hands of women, in which case the very concept of "domina-tion" will disappear.

In the same sequence from the Epistle to Henry II Nostradamus gives us further hints to this end.

> *The other child, who, to his great confusion and late*
> *repentance, will want to ruin her, will be involved in*
> *three widely different areas, namely the Roman,*
> *Germany and Spain, which will arrange different*
> *kinds of armed forces.*
>
> —The Epistle to Henry II[45]

The "other child," in our present frame of reference, probably refers to the third child, who caused some consternation in his dealings with the world. He achieves first *confusion*, and then *repentance*, which in Nostradamus's terms is a good process. Within the Catholic tradition, sin followed by repentance is almost better than no sin in the first place! So our third child of the feminine spirit is the prodigal son, who will be active in Italy, Germany, and Spain—close to where the second child was traveling across the Alps and the Pyrenees.

Here again, we may wish to abandon the literal interpretation and take hold of the broader, allegorical meaning.

> *The alliance between the United States and Europe*
> *may flounder at its start, but then result in*
> *something which will provide a new role for the*
> *armed forces.*

We have, perhaps for some time, been aware of the possibility that the world's armed forces might have a purpose other than that of fighting each other. It may just be that the armies of the major world powers could have the function of helping to keep peace among emergent nations.

There is little doubt that the patriarchal attitude of domination by fear will not suddenly disappear with the advent of a critical mass of women in power, and certainly not simply with the arrival of a female American president. So it is clear that the new woman president of the United States will still be dealing with the old values of society, which include the need for armed forces that might help to control troubled nations such as strife-torn Yugoslavia.

What we may be looking at is the feminine influence bringing about a global police authority that will *arrange different kinds of armed forces.*

We may suppose that the sons and daughters of our first female American president are influential in this process.

The story continues:

And everything will pay attention to the ancient religions related to the regions of Europe north of the 48th parallel. These will have trembled to begin with its timidity, but thereafter the areas to the west, south and east will also tremble. But the nature of their power will be such that co-operation will work better than war.

One of the most convincing aspects of Nostradamus's prophecies is the fact that there is such consistency within and between the different works. It may not seem so to the casual reader, but once the verses and writings of this extraordinary prophet are examined in more detail, there arise numerous instances when one part of the work backs up another.

This is the case in these lines. First, we hear again the word "cooperation," which we may take to signal a complete change in attitude. Second, we learn that there is an important influence in the form of ancient religions, as we had learned before when Nostradamus told us of "pagan" religions and sects. It may be fair to suggest that as the organized religious belief systems become less reliable, and as people turn more to the personal side of religion—as is already happening in the early twenty-first century, when cult religions have offered more, and freer, possibilities than for a long time—so small, "cult-type" religious belief systems will grow in popularity.

> But the nature of their power will be such that co-operation will better than war.

This is perhaps the most significant line in the whole piece—that there will be attempts to resolve differences through cooperation rather than conflict.

If the new female president achieves this, she will have done more than any past male president of the United States.

To sum up the story so far, according to this interpretation of the Epistle to Henry II:

We can expect to see a female candidate win the United States presidential election in the year 2000.

This individual may be Ann Richards, Barbara Boxer, or another female candidate living in the south of the country.

Whoever she is, her four offspring will play a major part in the world's political and religious future, in particular in relation to a stronger alliance between the United States and Europe.

This may also be seen as an allegorical presentation of the furtherance of the feminist movement in the United States and Europe, where these four individuals play a determining role in the way that human relations improve.

A world policing force will grow out of the United States–Europe alliance. And as a result of this new view of politics, cooperation will be a key word.

Mainstream religion will take a greater account of small sect-oriented belief systems.

And, to be remembered from an earlier chapter, the female presidency will run into problems around three decades after it has begun, say in the beginning of the third decade of the twenty-first century.

All this will occur from about 1996, through 2000, and up to approximately the year 2030.

2009 FAMILY FORTUNES

The Royal scepter will have to accept that which his predecessors have employed. Because they do not understand the ring when they come to destroy the palace.

—C7 V23[1]

Approximately two out of every three U.S. marriages end in divorce. Two-thirds of the adults you see in the streets have gone through at least one marriage that has failed. This is not taking into account that many more couples today simply don't get married in the first place.[2]

The problems that the English royal couple suffered in the mid- to late 1990s exemplify the often unsatisfactory process of formal marriage. Nostradamus uses the example of Charles and Diana as part of his commentary on the social tradition of binding love affairs with legal and religious knots. The last words of this strange quatrain also appear to refer to the death of Diana in Paris.

Nevertheless, particularly in the United States, there has been a great resurgence in enthusiasm for family security, as though somehow we are running for shelter amid all the uncertainties inherent in this era. Paired with this, however, are important new changes happening in family life, brought about partly by the astrological presence of the planet Pluto, which tends to cause poisons to rise to the surface wherever it appears. The apparent instance of child abuse and physical abuse between men and women has become greater. This emphasis on the negative aspects of relationships results in deeper changes. If the truth is not known, how can change take place?

On the grand scale of astrology, we have lived within the characteristics of the Piscean Age for two thousand years, and are now entering the Age of Aquarius. This in itself produces massive transformations in the way our lives are led and accounts for changes in attitude on many levels.

Aquarius is concerned with friendship and partnership more than with sexuality and the body. Ideas as opposed to reality are of central importance. As we've seen in earlier chapters, the subjects of physics today are largely based on ideas rather than reality. Quantum theory was just that, not quantum reality. Scientists who propose ideas such as string theory will then spend years trying to prove it.

Plato taught us that there are first and foremost divine concepts, of which the world is a reflection. For the Aquarius, this is the perfect way to live, and as a result we are seeing a strong return to spiritual ideas, to "new" ideas about God, though in truth they are no more than new forms of the same old ideas. Even sexuality for the Aquarian is mostly about fantasy, anticipation, experimentation, health, and so on. There is little concern for the hard or soft basic physical experience. In the Piscean Age the most important element of sex was for it to be forbidden. The British Victorians loved most of all to pre-vent sexuality in order to give it tension and excitement, as do fundamental Christians, the Islamic faith, Catholics, and many of the minor cult religions. The monastic concept of celibacy is based in reality on the forbidden nature of sexuality. There are still monasteries in parts of Europe that will not allow their monks even to look upon a female, even a baby girl! All this vanishes in the future Aquarian Age, as we become more interested in understanding than in pretending. This in turn changes the way family life is set up.

In this new age of understanding there will be a greater interest in communal care for children, thus opening up the nuclear family into something broader and, in the end, proba-bly safer. The sometimes claustrophobic elements of the tight four-member family unit will be dispersed by local community care. Architecture may even begin to reflect these changes. Buildings like Le Corbusier's "Radial City" or like the Spanish *Corale*, where several homes are built around a central open space in which families gather, may become popular.[3]

And relationships will be less concerned with marriage as the civilized world becomes disillusioned with organized reli-gion and also realizes that marriage, more often than not, doesn't work anyway.

2009 COMPUTERS AND THE INTERNET: FASTER AND FASTER AND FASTER

Suffering past, the world is made smaller, peace
inhabits the populated earth: it will be possible to
communicate securely by many new methods,
though conflict will return.

—C1 V63[1]

There will be greater order in the world, and hope
for a century recovered from the sinister past, those
that have caused problems will change for the better,
and from the new fire of communication, few will
remain unaffected.

—C2 V10[2]

In the 1940s, IBM's first chairman, Thomas Watson, predicted a world market for "maybe five computers."[3] By 1975, about fifty thousand were operating, and in 1997 more than 140 million. Add to that the 170 million computers on credit cards currently in use worldwide. And that does not take into account the "invisible computers" built into routine appliances: A typical car today contains more computer-processing power than the first lunar landing craft in 1969.[4]

The reason for this explosive proliferation is simple: never has the world seen as vertiginous a drop in the price of an industrial product. We have gotten used to the idea that today's $2,000 laptop packs more power than the $10 million mainframe of twenty years ago. If car efficiency had followed the same trend, you would now drive across the United States on a fraction of a drop of gasoline.

When steam power was introduced, it was not all that much cheaper than water power, and it took from 1790 to 1850 to halve its real price. Likewise, it took from 1890 to 1930 for the price of electricity to drop by just over half. Contrast that with the cost of computing power, which halves every eighteen months. ("Moore's law," named after the president of Intel, actually describes a rate in which computational speed doubles *and* the price drops by half every eighteen months.)[5]

Just one facet of it—the Internet—is the topic of an estimated twelve thousand articles *per month* in the U.S. press alone. This, of course, does not include what is written on the Internet about the Internet itself. Never before has any technological shift been heralded by such an avalanche. George Gilder calls it "the biggest technological juggernaut that ever rolled."[6] Bill Gates, the founder of Microsoft, claims that "the benefits and problems arising from the Internet Revolution will be much greater than those brought about by the PC revolution."[7] Again, gigantic drops in cost and rise in speed are driving the change.

The Information Revolution is definitely the most self-conscious revolution that has ever occurred. Although skepticism is healthy when faced with this much hype, this revolution could yet prove a real one. It is clearly the opinion of the stock market: by early 1997, the combined stock market value of Microsoft and Intel ($274 billion) comfortably exceeded the combined value of General Motors, Ford, Boeing, Eastman Kodak, Sears, J.P. Morgan, Caterpillar, and Kellogg ($235 billion).[8]

Whole libraries have been written about the "gee-whiz" technologies involved. Even if we focus only on money on the Net, the topics of new payment systems and the implications of cryptography for cybermoney definitely warrant an entire book. Instead of taking that route, let us focus here only on the meaning of this Information Revolution and the opportunity it represents for choosing our money systems in the near future.

According to inventor Ray Kurzweil in his book *The Age of the Spiritual Machines*, by the early part of the twenty-first century computers will be performing a trillion calculations per second, and it will be possible for anyone with $1,000 to own one.[9] These incredible machines will fit into jewelry worn on the body, and laptops will be no more than the size of a small, thin book. Access without any kind of cable connection will be normal, with shortwave radio transmitters connecting us to the Web, and continuous speech recognition replacing our need to type on a keyboard. Telephones will translate between languages automatically. And this is just the beginning of an age that most of us will sample firsthand.

By 2019, the same $1,000 (in 1999 terms) will buy a machine equal to the computing capability of the human brain. Not only this, but the machines will be so small as to be virtually invisible, hidden in clothing, furniture, and the walls themselves. We will communicate between one another and the Web via 3-D virtual-display units in our reading glasses, contact lenses, and wristwatches, and spoken language will do the work of instructing these minuscule devices, including home heating systems, two-way instant communication, and library downloading.

It will no longer be necessary to be in the physical presence of another to see, hear, or touch him. Virtual reality, and "realistic all-encompassing tactile environments," will enable us to do almost anything with anyone we please (presumably with their consent).

Even getting around from one place to another will happen with automated vehicle systems gridlocked to the road systems everywhere. Driving accidents will therefore become virtually impossible. As Nostradamus so adeptly writes: "Suffering past, the world is made smaller, peace inhabits the populated earth: it will be possible to communicate securely by many new methods . . ."

By 2029, the same $1,000 will buy you a computer with a thousand times the capacity of the human brain. We'll be thinking faster than we have ever thought before! Even if you're fifty now, you will more than likely share in this extraordinary revolution given the fact, as discussed earlier, that homegrown organs, bones, and other parts of the body will bring about "a chance for death to end." An eighty-year-old may well have decades and even perhaps centuries left to live. And that formerly old-aged individual will have computers scattered about his or her whole body—to enhance hearing, sight, touch, physical energy, sensitivity, and even sexual capacity.

Computers will have "read" all available human literature and information so that the brain-implanted biochip will be able to access anything anywhere at the simple input of a thought transmitted by instant wave contact. Information will flow continuously throughout the planet and between all humans at all times. The problem will not be finding the answers but shutting them out: "from the new fire of communication, few will remain unaffected."

If you think an increase from 500 MHz computing speed to 1,000 MHz is a big jump, imagine a computer running at 60 qubits—that is, managing a million trillion simultaneous solutions. This is quantum computing and will be possible before halfway through the next century.

And, of course, along with this massive change in our lifetimes, the biggest effect will be on the Internet. By 2009 people will have effectively become portable computers, with as many as ten computers on or around their bodies. These tiny chip components will be networked using "body LANs," or local area networks, and linked with worldwide webs providing cellular phone facilities, pagers, automated identity services, and contact with information anywhere in the world. They will work with electronic memories and will not need keyboards—hard drives will be a feature of past. Virtually everything at this time will be organized through shortwave wireless technology.

The entertainment industry will be one of the single biggest users of the Internet, as it is now. According to surveys, more than a billion dollars were spent on sexually explicit Web sites during 1998.[10] By 2009 it will be possible to interact on the Web with virtual touch and an all-enveloping technology that will simulate sexual contact with others or with imaginary virtual beings. Virtual sex will be both safer and probably more stimulating than real sexuality because it will include physical experiences that do not even exist today. Further, virtual sex will not be monitored. And, as virtual sex will be completely safe and personal to users, all forms of prostitution will certainly be legal as well. This will probably also apply to less savory forms of sexual indulgence. In this, Nostradamus seems to have seen the future: "though conflict will return."

The Web will also provide virtual experiences such as spiritual realizations. It is already clear from recent experiments that the brain and body can be stimulated electronically to create a wide range of realities. Even laughter can be found in the depths of the synapses. In experiments undertaken at UCLA, reported in *Nature* (May 1999), neurological triggers were stimulated in the supplementary motor area of the brain that made the subject guffaw with laughter. The subject, when stimulated in this area, found everything that went on around her hilariously funny, regardless of whether it might have been funny to an unstimulated subject.[11]

As the computer, at least by this time, will already have both a complete record of the DNA of the human being and a total comprehension of the brain's synapse systems, there is little doubt that experiences available on the Web will range from the lowest to the highest, all the way to a spiritual contact with God. Certain crude chemical substances can arrange for an individual to experience spiritual satori. The Web will do it perhaps without harm or side effects. Addiction may be available still, but with less risk to the body and mind. A group at the University of California has discovered what it calls the "God Module," a tiny group of nerve cells in the frontal lobe of the brain that seems to be most active during religious and spiritual awareness.[12] We are but a series of electronics and chemicals, after all, even at the "highest" levels of our awareness, and although this may seem sacrilegious, it is perhaps the start of a more sober view of religion, which might in turn prevent the unpleasant side effects of interdenominational conflict. Here again, however, Nostradamus understands mankind's passion for passion: "though conflict will return."

2010 THE END OF FEAR

Eyes closed, opened by antique imagination,
The habits of those alone will be brought to nothing:
The great monarch will chastise their frenzy,
Attacking the treasures before the temples.
The body without soul no longer to be sacrificed:
Deaths day will be birthday:
The divine spirit will make the soul happy,
Seeing the word in its eternity.

—C2 V11–12[1]

One of the most important transforming powers of the women's movement, which is of great value to the future, is the ability to end fear.

If there is one aspect of the patriarchal system that has done the greatest damage, it is the engendering of an almost inherent fearfulness within us all.

We are not talking about the kind of fear that causes us to jump out of the way of a speeding car or avoid contact with an angry lion. This is not so much fear as the need to survive—a kind of physical reflex that arises from a million years of conditioning.

The fear we are discussing here is the existential fear that arises in the absence of love or light. For thousands of years now we have been under the influence of religions that are essentially fear-driven: Christianity, Judaism, Islam, Hinduism. If you are sinful, you will not go to heaven. If you do not obey the law, you will be destroyed. If you behave in a certain "evil" way during this life, you will suffer during the next.

The original concept behind these absurd ideas was to help people whose lives were disastrously unhappy anyway. If you lived in huts or tents or on the street, and had no food to eat, no one who loved you, no place to go, these religions provided you with something simple to keep you going. There was a prospect of "heaven," even if it was only after death. At least there was something to hope for. If you lived without sin (whatever that is), you might be happy after you die. But now, thousands of years after all this was created, we still think in terms of being "God-fearing," as though this were a good thing. And this God-fearing attitude colors all aspects of our lives.

After thousands of years of conditioning, we believe in this punitive God on a level that we can no longer access or change. Essentially what this belief has done is to put out the light, leaving us mostly in the dark. The underlying basis for it is redundant in most Western countries because now we have luxury, most of us are loved by someone, we live regular, secure lives, and we often have the opportunity to live in heaven right now, if we could just stop complaining for a moment. But still we carry this unconscious fear around with us as though it were essential to our lives. It takes the form of continuous worrying, fear of losing control of our lives, fear of tomorrow, fear of losing the job, the girlfriend, the house, fear of death.

As the patriarchal "atmosphere" disperses with the arrival of a critical mass of women, basic and essential aspects of our lives will be transformed. This is why it is so important that women become our political leaders, our religious leaders, our mother goddesses again.

We began chapter 6 with a single verse that told us about the order that will result in the next century from the arrival of a greater feminine spirit. This quatrain is followed by three more that continue the story, two of which are set out at the beginning of this prediction. There follows now a free interpretation of all four verses.

Before long everything will be rearranged. We can expect a very strange century. Women's estate that was masked and alone will change everything. Few will wish to remain the way they were.

The next son of the important one will become powerful in the realm of the privileged and everyone will be afraid of his greed. But his disciples will be thrown out. Eyes that were closed will be opened by an ancient understanding. The aura and environment of those who have been alone will be proven pointless, and the religious leaders and those that have an investment in continuing fear will chastise the enthusiasm of the rest, putting the newfound treasure down as useless.

It will be shown that the body is not important because the soul always continues, and death will be regarded as the same as birth. The understanding

that the spirit is divine will make everyone joyful,
because they will see the truth on a broader level.

This is no mean piece of prophecy, and it exemplifies the extraordinary capability and understanding of this enigmatic man. The story he tells us is of the arrival of a new force that has hitherto been masked. We are interpreting this as meaning women's estate, and that upon the arrival of this estate everything will be reordered and everyone will quickly realize what problems had previously been caused by patriarchy. Life is like that. We have a tendency to labor on in conditions that are not ideal because we cannot conceive of anything different. We complain continuously, but do nothing to change the situation. And then something happens and we find ourselves in a new situation that is better for us. What a relief! If only it had happened earlier.

Such is the change that Nostradamus describes. But a major part of this transformation is that we learn to throw out the old habits and adopt a new approach.

And that new way is religious, as is so much of our fundamental nature.

Eyes that were closed will be opened by an ancient
understanding . . .

Ancient religious understanding is already gaining greater importance than it has had for centuries. In the United States and some European countries, paganism, or neopaganism, has become so popular that there are even sects that have adopted the ancient ideals of natural harmony, love of the environment, the ancient goddesses and brought them to the forefront again. These old understandings will become new again, according to our prophet.

Nostradamus next uses the fear surrounding loneliness as his metaphor for the change. What he is telling us is that we will not need to fear being alone, or unloved, because the new belief systems of the feminine order will help everyone to accept the human condition in its real and natural form. There are already many groups of people gathering together to take advantage, for example, of the Buddhist philosophies, which are so much more supportive of human nature and less concerned to be critical of sexual attitudes and needs—aspects of human nature that have been put down so vehemently by the Christian faiths. There are also numerous smaller religious groups, that we may choose to call cults, that are creating new ways of living based on ancient religions from the East. All this is part of the change that humanity so badly needs.

The traditional religious leaders will attempt to dampen the new spirit, but will not succeed. And in the last lines we get the point of it all:

It will be shown that the body is not important because the soul always continues, and death will be regarded as the same as birth. The understanding that the spirit is divine will make everyone joyful, because they will see the truth on a broader level.

Essentially we will discover that life is eternal, and there is nothing to stop us all from being joyful. NOW. We will discover that we do not need to fear death because it is only another life transition, and if we do not fear death then there is no need to worry about what tomorrow will bring.

Perhaps all this sounds hugely idealistic and too hopeful, but maybe the future really could be a better place, and our pessimism only arises out of the patriarchal conditioning that we have suffered for so long.

2011 ANIMALS AND CHIPS

. . . and from the new fire of communication, few will remain unaffected.

—C2 V10[1]

Scientists working with the military in Germany and the United States were already, in the last years of the old millennium, working on tiny computer chips to be installed into the brains of animals. When Nostradamus tells us that "few will remain unaffected," he really means it! These bionic computerized creatures are planned for use as controlled "soldiers" to be used by armed forces to do the kind of reconnaissance previously undertaken by humans. They would be employed in frontline work to search dangerous areas of terrain and hunt for victims of war and signal collapsed buildings. They might also search for mines and reconnoiter enemy positions.

The computer chips embedded in the animals' brains would provide the operators with control through radio wave technology, and tiny cameras mounted on the bodies would operate to send back visual information. The sophistication of these devices is increasing exponentially with experiments that allow scientists to grow brain cells onto microchips that can be operated to detect nerve gases. These experiments, undertaken at the Naval Research Laboratory in Washington, D.C., currently only on animals, could eventually be used to control a whole species of animals and, of course, in our worst fears—of humans.[2] In the future, all kinds of exciting and perhaps frightening developments could result from the implanting and growing of neurons onto computer chips so small as to be barely detectable.

As of now the plans include the use of rats to check out the results of bombing damage in industrial areas without raising any suspicion of their potential "spying" presence. Dogs would work well in battle areas to search for casualties or to discover pilots who have bailed out of crashed airplanes.

No one in the animal rights sectors of any civilized country is going to applaud such use of the innocent of our animal kingdom, but the temptation is certainly going to be present. Human beings will certainly make use of these minuscule, even microscopic, electronic units in the new millennium, but more likely for things that bring pleasure and excitement than for activities that threaten.

2012 HOW MANY HUMANS?

The change will be very hard. Cities and countries will gain by the growth, with good intentions, prudence, and cunning there will be results and across the world the culture will change because of it.
—*C4 V21*[1]

Earlier we touched on the problems of a growing population in relation to climate and food shortages, at least as seen through the eyes of Nostradamus. Here we examine overpopulation on the ground, so to speak.

The question of the rapid growth of human population is now cliché. It is such a prevalent problem, cited for so long as a problem for the future, that we hardly give it consideration in our everyday lives. Nostradamus, however, wrote about it several times. As he says in the verse above, "cities and countries will gain by the growth." Society and religion want to fuel growth, while people themselves are overwhelmed by the crowded streets in cities like London and Tokyo, where it is already impossible to find quiet spaces, and private and public transportation have become a nightmare. When disasters like the Yugoslavian/Kosovo debacle occur, a shift in population caused by fleeing refugees overwhelms surrounding nations and their ability to absorb large numbers of people suddenly. In the future, we can see this kind of situation happening on a regular basis, as almost all areas of the planet will be bursting with too many people.

The planet's total population in the first years of the new millennium is approximately 6.2 billion.[2] That is an average of about 120 people for every square mile of the entire planet. By 2010, one billion more people are expected to be born than will die. That makes a total of 7.2 billion—a conservative estimate.

Just to give a little perspective, we might look into our past. In 1825, when population growth first became a field of study owing to Thomas Robert Malthus (*www.econlib.org/library/Malthus/malPlog.html*), who compiled a study entitled *Essay on the Principle of Population*, there were one billion people on earth. It had taken thousands of years to reach this momentous number. Improvements in medical care and the Industrial Era were causing population to accelerate, and in the next hundred years the figure doubled to two billion and then doubled again in the following fifty years to four billion in 1976.[3]

Since 1990, the growth rate has slowed down slightly owing to a reduction in the fertility rate in the Western civilized world, but we won't really feel the effect of this for some time, as population growth changes are rather like an oil tanker—it takes a long time to speed up and slow down. In fact, there will not be a leveling of human population growth to the point where only the same number of people are born as die before the middle of the twenty-first century. By that time there could be around fifteen billion people on earth. As mentioned before, that's nearly three times as many people on the planet as there are today.

Population growth will not, of course, occur evenly across the whole planet. Some groups will grow faster than others. Take the United States, a country with a wide cross section of different races. During 1994 there were approximately 218 million white people in the country, 33 million black people, 27 million Hispanic people, 9.4 million Asians, and 2.4 million Native Americans. In the year 2000 there were 227 million whites (a 3.6 percent increase), 36 million black people (a 7.2 percent increase), 32 million Hispanic people (a 17 percent increase), and 12 million Asians (a 23 percent increase), while the Native American population remained stable. Between 2000 and 2050 whites will grow by only a further 26 percent, while the number of black people will grow 73 percent, Hispanic people by 182 percent, Asians by 234 percent, and Native Americans by 100 percent.[4]

By halfway through the twenty-first century there will be about as many nonwhites as whites in the United States. This will also be reflected in other parts of the world, particularly China and India.

City Life

In the study of demographics, the pattern of movement in and out of cities (in terms of accommodation) is fascinating. During the early years of the twenty-first century, more people are expected to move into urban areas—"cities and countries will gain by the growth"—while the wealthy will run away from them. For those who live or work in cities today, the experiences of traffic jams, crime, overpopulation, parking, and general stress have become entirely familiar. Each year it becomes more difficult to reach our offices and homes, with drivers often growing into maniacs from the anxieties of attempting to maneuver the highways. The 1990s saw a remarkable increase in interest in retreats, faraway silent places, music that evokes tranquillity, and any information related to silence and remote spaces where we can escape the madness and noise of city life. This is a natural response to the greater instance of overcrowding in cities, but in reality the trend in the early years of the twenty-first century is to increase city populations still further.

City populations during the 1950s were typically as follows: New York City, 12.3 million people; London, 8.7 million; and Tokyo, 6.9 million; while Paris, Moscow, and Buenos Aires had 5 million each. By 1990, New York was outnumbered by 25 million in Tokyo, an increase of three times! New York had 16 million, London 10 million and *reducing*, while New Mexico had grown to 15 million and Buenos Aires tipped 11.4 million.[5]

The estimates for the year 2010 are that Tokyo will hit 30 million; Bombay, the second-largest city in the world by then, will be at another 25 million; and New York only at 17 million. The thirty largest cities in the world will house some 450 million people, nearly twice as many people as in the whole United States during the last years of the twentieth century. China and India will be by far the most densely populated countries in the world.[6]

The by-product of this lemming-like rush for urban life will be a rush away from the cities. By the early years of the next millennium, England, for example, will likely be one massive suburb!

Celebrations in London

And the story continues in the following verses. Nostradamus often wrote his quatrains in sequence, rather like a map of our future. In the section entitled "The End of Fear," the passages (*Century* 2: 10–13) revealed the possibility of a new understanding of life and death.

These lines were followed by a verse describing the transformation of the Catholic Church, which we discussed in the last section, "Moving the Stars and the Pope." Two verses after this we find the following:

> *Naples, Palermo, Sicily, Syracuse, New leaders,*
> *celestial lightning and fires, Power from London,*
> *Ghent, Brussels and Susa, Great slaughter, triumph*
> *leads to festivities.*
>
> —*C2 V16*[7]

It is suggested that this quatrain prophesies a collective response to a meteorite attack—that the combined military forces of many nations manage to stop or destroy the two massive rocks that were hurtling toward the planet, "slaughtering" them, and that this triumph leads to great celebrations.

This, on the face of it, shows us a great victory. But on a more subtle level it is a victory of a different kind. The world's military might would, in this case, have been used for the benefit of mankind, not to its disadvantage. Armies and weapons would have been employed to save humanity from death, rather than cause it.

This would be a cause for celebration. And certainly such a transformation would have a direct connection with a greater feminine presence in positions of political and religious power.

The military activity caused by the imminent arrival of two massive meteorites seems to center on southern Italy, north Africa, and other areas of Europe, including London and Ghent, Belgium, the country where the European Community has its administration. Interestingly, in Nostradamus's day, control of the Sultanate of Susa, in Tunisia, was being contested by Hapsburg Spain and the advancing Ottoman Empire. So we are being shown the rival worlds of Christendom and Islam uniting to triumph over an extraterrestrial threat.

The Strength of Weakness

Continuing in the same vein, we find another verse in this sequence that gives us a prediction of the natural consequence of a new view of cooperation—the disbanding of armies in a future governed by women.

> *The aimless army of Europe will depart, joining together close to the submerged island: The weakened fleet will fold up, At the navel of the world, a greater voice replacing it.*
>
> *—C2 V22[8]*

There are two indications in this quatrain that, in the light of earlier verses, specifically place it in our immediate future.

One of Nostradamus's earlier verses makes a famous prediction, which has been echoed by other prophets, including the modern American prophet Edgar Cayce. In this prophecy, part of England's south coast will sink into the sea because of a geological change. Nostradamus refers again to that prediction here. Cayce specifically states that this would occur at the end of the twentieth century or the beginning of the twenty-first.

Also, the last line of this verse repeats the prediction that the Pope will change locations—*At the navel of the world, a greater voice replacing it.* The "navel of the world" is probably an allegorical reference to Rome as the religious center of the world (at least from the perspective of Nostradamus's age).

So we are placing this event, concerning the European army, at approximately the same time as all the other events that are occurring because of the presence of a female American president and the greater power of the feminine spirit.

And the prediction is telling us that because of a lack of energy, an aimlessness, the European army will cease to exist and the weakened fleet (the Navy) will also fold up and pack its bags. And all this will come about because there is an overriding cause—*a greater voice replacing it.*

The general demobilization could, of course, be connected with the alliance we spoke of earlier between the United States and Europe, in which armies are redeployed to police the world. It could also flow from the experience of joint action in the face of external threat to the planet. It certainly suggests that in the future there will be less need for armies because wars will no longer be a regular event.

Whatever the cause, the result must be good. The fewer armies the better.

Disavowing the Old Habits

Naturally, with the development of a completely new paradigm, many of the old habits will become redundant. Some of
us may rue the day that our "normal" lives are disrupted, others will cheer that ancient, tired, and bored behavior will be
replaced with something fresh. This is another of the characteristics of women—they invariably cause the world to have to
change. Once they are put into positions of power in greater
numbers there will be no standing still, even for a moment.

And one of these changes is outlined in a strange, enigmatic verse:

> *When the adulterer who is wounded without a blow*
> *being struck, he will have murdered his wife and*
> *son out of frustration: wife knocked over he will*
> *strangle the child.*
>
>   —*C8 V63*[9]

This piece of prophecy is one of those found scattered
throughout the writings of Nostradamus that we might call
"prophecies of general change." Put another way, they appear,
usually as single verses, as though Nostradamus were simply
commenting by the wayside. Traveling along through the
events of the centuries, he pauses every so often to make a
general comment about conditions of life at some particular
moment. This verse seems to tell us something about the state
of marriage and its effect on the family unit.

As the feminine spirit moves forward during the next century, entirely different conditions will evolve. Once women are

no longer forced—through their parents' ideas and condition-ing—to become wives, family makers, and mothers, but are free to choose whether to do this or not, the whole family structure will have to change. Women may still wish to stay at home and raise children, but they may also wish to bear chil-dren and have the men stay at home and father them. This happened in the latter years of the twentieth century, but in the future it will become even more common, affecting the way we see our marital structures.

There may even be happier and more fulfilling ways for children to be born. Once we have finally broken free of all the complications attendant on organized religion, and become practical about life and death, the mores surrounding mar-riage and birth will be transformed into something more real-istic. We may abandon the idea of marriage as a religious vow altogether. This is not to say that people will not continue to be married—if that makes us happy, why not? But already, during this century, the estate of marriage has changed dra-matically because of the greatly increased instance of divorce. For many of us marriage is no more than a romantic idea, and does not need to become a prison.

In the verse we are looking at here, Nostradamus suggests that adultery and marriage have wounded the heart— *wounded without a blow being struck*—and that the man, through frustration, "murders" the wife and child. This could be seen to be a description of how families can develop into states of pain and violence.

But as we have seen, it is now possible for women to stand up and be heard on the often tender and painful subject of family problems. As we mentioned in an earlier chapter, television programs such as the *Oprah Winfrey Show* have given women a voice and the knowledge that their voice is actually being listened to and acted upon. This has been immensely valuable in the evolution of the feminine spirit and will lead to women refusing to accept what they are hurt by and refusing to be dominated by frustrated and poorly conditioned men. In turn, men will change their attitudes toward women, and many of the old prejudices will begin to disappear.

What we find in Nostradamus's overall vision of the future of women during the next two decades is a radical paradigm shift in the quality of life, brought about by a much stronger and more revolutionary movement on the part of women than might have been expected during our times.

There is a tendency among conservative male groups to suggest that the feminist movement has been militant enough and that men are already changing to accommodate the demands of women. But Nostradamus indicates that the movement has hardly even begun. It is natural, as we have seen, for the habit of patriarchy to stick. It is also normal for a very considerable critical mass to be needed to shift anything that has been an established habit for so long. We could not have expected, for example, to change the attitudes of certain groups of white people toward black people, or the entrenched prejudice against homosexual love, without major upheaval. These changes are still occurring and have had to pass through long periods of difficulty for the paradigm shift to occur. But the patriarchal prejudice against the feminine is older and far more entrenched, being the result of millennia of thoughtless violence and suppression.

We can expect, therefore, a great deal more upheaval associated with feminism, and the balance of power between the sexes, than we have hitherto experienced. And if we believe in Nostradamus's capacity to predict the future, the first major move to this end will be the Seline March, which will occur during the winter of the year that the comet Chiron is visible from Earth. This will be followed by the greater political presence of a certain woman in American political life and her election in the millennial year.

Nostradamus prophesies that humanity will be led thereafter into a happier and more harmonious future, flowing from an acceptance of the rightful place of the feminine in all our lives.

2013–2014 THE EARLY 2000s: AIDS, FULL REALIZATION

Social Disease

One of the most profound ways in which mankind has expressed his inner poisons over the years around the end of this century is through human diseases. In his epistle to Henry II, Nostradamus had the following to say about the last years of Pluto's transition.

> *The leaders of the Church will be backward in their love for God. Of the three sects the Catholic is thrown into decadence by the partisan differences of its worshippers. The Protestant will be entirely undone in all Europe and part of Africa by the Islamics, by means of poor in spirit who, led by madmen (terrorists), shall through worldly luxury commit adultery. In the meantime so vast a plague that two-thirds of the world will fail and decay. So many that no one will know the true owners of fields and houses. The weeds in the city streets will rise higher than the knees, and there shall be a total desolation of the Clergy.*[1]

The rising panic surrounding the spread of AIDS is more than familiar to us all. If the published statistics are anything to go by, more than a million people in America alone are already confirmed as being infected with the virus. If there is no cure, or at least a profound change in public attitudes and behavior, the figures could be well into the tens of millions by the end of the first decade of the new millennium, along with vast portions of the population in some African and Asian countries. Given his tendency to exaggerate, Nostradamus's prediction that two-thirds of the human race would be killed by a plague could be not so far from the truth. But perhaps the predicted plague is not simply that of AIDS, but something far more widespread and more deeply rooted.

It should be remembered that the time of Nostradamus was a time of plague also. The bubonic plague swept through Europe from China during the fifteenth and sixteenth centuries in such a way that people believed the whole world would be dead within a few years. The bubonic and pneumonic plagues are still around in the twenty-first century. In fact, reports in 2000 from California showed that the squirrels and rats in the forests around San Francisco and Los Angeles were carrying the plague in large numbers. A schoolteacher actually died of the plague in the 1990s. It took less than one day from the showing of the symptoms to her death. AIDS is not like that. Its growth is much more a mirror of our age. It is enigmatic, changing in shape, and sexually related. The moment one strain of it has been discovered, the structure of the disease appears to change into a different form and attack again. It is as though we have spawned a disease to beat all diseases, except that this sickness is still more complex even than this, for it is not made up of one labeled disease called AIDS but several, like a lethal cocktail.

The Multiplague

On the doorstep of and inside two cities, there will
be two pestilences like none ever seen. Hunger,
inside pestilence, except for iron, they will be at the
end, crying for help to the great immortal God.[2]

There are many verses among the *Centuries* that predict the coming of a great plague. Each age looks on these predictions as representing a particular disease that will ultimately wipe out mankind or at least the greater part of the race of humanity. In Nostradamus's age the great plague was bubonic. After the World Wars, the great plague was cancer. In our age, at the beginning of the twenty-first century, the plague to beat all plagues is AIDS. But this all seems very subjective. We are not seeing our world through the eyes of the Prophet himself, but through our own fearfulness. It is true that AIDS is a terrible killer and may already have infected a far larger area of population than we realize. But it seems more likely that Nostradamus was seeing something far wider in its influence, something that has a stronger root in the very foundations of society and particularly now in the United States.

We could call this plague something completely new. We could call it the "multiplague" because it appears to be made up of several different parts. The basic components of this social epidemic are *(1)* the HIV virus; *(2)* syphilis or some similar venereal component; *(3)* poverty; *(4)* depression;

(5) drug abuse; *(6)* ignorance and prejudice. It is not that these different conditions are independent of one another, because in recent surveys done within U.S. hospitals and university laboratories it appears that they all feed off one another. The existence of extreme poverty causes despondency that leads to clinical depression. Poor diet exacerbates this condition. Poor diet is made worse, in turn, by media advertising, for it is the poor-quality foods that are more vociferously advertised, particularly on television, the twenty-first century's ultimate escape mechanism. Depression through poverty and poor diet leads to smoking, alcoholism, and drug abuse. The excessive abuse of drugs then leads to further poverty, and through either a contaminated needle or unprotected sexual relations, the HIV virus is contracted, very often along with syphilis. Syphilis is more rampant in the United States during the early 2000s than it has been since the eighteenth and nineteenth centuries in Europe.[3] To finally cap the problem, particularly in relation to attitudes toward the gay communities, there is ignorance and prejudice that in the United States has led to a reluctance on the part of the government to put sufficient funds into research for cures. In a hospital in the South Bronx in New York City in 1999, 38 percent of adults tested were HIV-positive. More than 250,000 cases of the AIDS virus were confirmed during 1999 in New York City alone, making that city a threat to the world, as it contains a highly mobile population.[4]

In effect, the HIV virus, syphilis, drugs, and social deprivations are feeding off one another and building an epidemic that could become the killer that Nostradamus foresaw. And the root of this epidemic is not only medical but also social, economic, and political, also emotional and psychological. It is true that the advent of AIDS in the United States is seen as having derived through the gay community, who are not generally a poor community. The progress of AIDS since inception has developed into poverty-stricken areas, and essentially the cure will not be only a medical cure, for this is simply like shifting around the deck chairs on the *Titanic*. The moment we find a vaccine for AIDS, another combination of the multi-plague will pop up right behind it, with similar prejudices and nearsightedness. The cure lies in a change of the whole structure of life, and America is the guinea pig.

2015 THE END OF DEPRESSION

Mars threatens with its warlike power, seventy wars will cause blood to flow. The fall and ruin of the clergy and more also for those who have no interest in them. The scythe joined to the pond towards Sagittarius at the height of its ascendant, plague, famine, death by military hand heralds the approach of the new century. For forty years the Iris will not appear, for forty more it will be seen every day. Then the earth will grow drier and great floods will occur when it is visible.[1]

Nostradamus concocted his prophecies, divining the "images" in his mind through various magical, occult devices; writing them down the following morning with the help of his assistant, Chavigny; turning them into enigmatic verses; then mixing them up. The author's effort here has been to crack the code of the jumbled verses and make some temporal sense of them. Sequences do exist, and many more of them have been revealed. But in some cases, Nostradamus left the verses in the sequence, presumably, that he had put them at the beginning. He did so with the three verses above, verses that reveal the most extraordinary events in our future.

To further unravel this remarkable poetic prophecy—
which we examined in brief earlier—we will start with the timing of the events he describes. This is provided by the astrological reference to the "scythe and the pond at the ascendant
of Sagittarius." The last time this occurred was in 1985. It
occurs again around the beginning of the new millennium,
then, on January 16, 2015, giving us a precise beginning for
something rather momentous that may take place in most of
the lives of those who read this book. We do not know, of
course, whether the date applied here is correct, as with all of
Nostradamus's prophecies; so have included both interpretations. The first is in the chapter on overpopulation and famine;
the second is here.

By this date we will have witnessed the fall of or a sub-
stantial change in the Roman Catholic Church. During the last
years of the twentieth century, we also saw plenty of "plague,
famine, death by military hand," right up to the madness of
Yugoslavia's Slobadan Milosevic in 1999. Nostradamus counts
seventy wars during the twentieth century—fairly close to the
truth.

If we follow the words, it is as though we actually transit
through time from the past into the future. From wars,
plagues, famine, dying religions, and insane politicians we
turn toward the Iris, which, according to most interpreters of
Nostradamus, the prophet uses in old French as deriving from
the Latin and Greek for the word *rainbow*. In Ancient Greece,
Iris was the goddess of the rainbow, and her job was to bring
water from the River Styx so that the gods could perform their
rituals. It would seem a natural assumption that he uses the
word *Iris* in this way, further applying rainbow to mean water

or rain. However, if we look only slightly more closely at the lines of the verses at the beginning of this chapter, we see that Nostradamus tells us that rain and lack of rain will occur at the same time! Unlikely, even in the supposed turmoil of a war-ravaged future. Perhaps the use of the word *Iris* was not intended to mean anything other than a flower.

The iris is derived from the family *Iridaceae*, of which there are some fifteen hundred species around the world. This group is well known for its curative powers, particularly the irises referred to in Latin as *florentina*, *pallida*, and *german-ica*, all of which are found in rich concentrations in southern France, where Nostradamus worked wonders as a medical doctor who used herbs to cure the ill during the bubonic plague. The dried material produced from the flowers is known as orrisroot, and once the oils are extracted from the flowers they can be used for perfumes and soaps, the remaining dried powder being applied largely as an antidepressant. (Nostradamus, the polymath and man of economy, also, incidentally, made special cosmetic potions and facial cleansers for the ladies of the French court.) If we reinterpret the last lines of the prophecy using this fresh knowledge, we may find a different future than the one most commonly asserted as having rain and drought occurring simultaneously.

Forty years before the end of the old millennium and perhaps into the beginning of the new millennium—forty years of depression, where no iris orrisroot was available to cure our sadness at the ghastly things individuals like Milosevic and others have managed to perpetrate out of their insanity. The iris becomes a metaphor for bad times. We then enter an era during which the iris is visible each day, a time when the world also enters the Aquarian Age, which promises a more peaceful and positive time for the human race.

Could this be the beginning of a Golden Age, an Age of the Iris? Could it be that there will be no apocalypse, no cataclysm greater than that which we have already experienced during the last warring century? Could it be that the arrival of the Messiah and the end of the world were no more than metaphors created by Christians?

2016–2020 THE GOLDEN AGE

*After that Antichrist will be the infernal prince again,
for the last time. All Kingdoms of Christianity will
tremble, even those of the infidels (Islam), for the
space of twenty-five years. Wars and battles will be
more grievous and towns, cities, castles, and all other
edifices will be burned, desolated, and destroyed, with
great effusion of vestal blood, violations of married
women and widows, and suckling children dashed
and broken against the walls of towns. By means of
Satan, Prince Infernal, so many evils will be commit-
ted that nearly all the world will find itself undone
and desolated. Before these events, some rare birds
will cry in the air: Today, today, and some time later
vanish. After this has endured for a long time, there
will be almost renewed another reign of Saturn, and a
golden age. Hearing the affliction of his people, God
the creator will command that Satan be cast into the
depths of the bottomless pit, and bound there. Then a
universal peace will commence between God and
man, and Satan will remain bound for around a
thousand years, and then all unbound.*

—Epistle to Henry II[1]

If we take Nostradamus too seriously, especially when we read prophecies such as the one above, we might imagine that our planet is on a downward spiral into apocalypse and hell. Seen from the prophet's perspective, the twentieth century must certainly have looked like a difficult time. We might face the fact that with two world wars, Vietnam, the war in Korea, Iraq, Bosnia, and Yugoslavia, plus a number of terrible conflicts in other parts of the planet, humanity has managed to make a pretty mess of things. We could say, therefore, that Nostradamus wasn't far wrong in his assessment of our time. As human beings during this time, conditioned to expect the worst and familiar with the almost perpetual state of having wars fought around us, we have a tendency to see this enigmatic prophet as being nothing other than a doom-monger. But in truth, the reverse, however, is true. Numerous verses contain more positive predictions, including, for example, the last lines of the above section of his letter to Henry II, where he tells us of a golden age we can expect to begin in the early part of the twenty-first century. Nostradamus says this coming era is one of "universal peace," and that it lasts a thousand years, then falls back to times of further conflict. This prophecy is echoed in the Bible's Book of Revelation, in which Saint John the Divine writes of a time when Satan will leave the planet for a thousand years.

A letter the prophet wrote to his son expresses the same concept: "For according to the celestial signs, the Golden Age will return, and after all calculations, with the world near to an all-encompassing revolution . . . this will be after the visible judgment of heaven, before we reach the millennium which shall complete all."[2]

This passage outlines fairly precisely what Nostradamus saw for the millennium we enter now. In earlier prophecies he provides a kind of history of the future, his future, the world we have lived through since his time. This ranges through some remarkably precise dating of events, including the beginning of the French Revolution, times of world war, and the lives of Hitler and other familiar characters. The holocaust of World War II is documented with incredible precision, and we can see through our own knowledge of our past history that for Nostradamus all this might well look like a terrible apocalyptic period. His prophecies of the growth of the United States to world power, the ending of Communism in the Soviet Union, and other major political events demonstrate the accuracy of the prophet's vision to a point where we might dare imagine he was right about a golden age in our future—the history of our future.

How strange such a time will be for us! So familiar are we with conflict and suffering, it would probably take the human race some time and effort to learn to live in peace.

2020–2025 HOW MONEY MIGHT BE

. . . an urn of gold is found and then restored.[1]

Let's imagine ourselves in an idyllic year 2020, looking back at the first years of the twenty-first century as a time that resolved all the differences in currency exchanges, inflation, and business booms and being able to say we managed to figure it all out in the end. Imagine that we have settled into an evolving complementary currency system. Almost all corporations and many individuals are dealing routinely in currencies at different levels, and exchanging on the Net for a small transaction fee has become simple.

Here is a résumé, according to Bernard Lietaer in *The Future of Money*,[2] of the four levels that could be operational in 2020:

- global corporate scrip
- regional currencies
- national currencies
- complementary currencies

Global Corporate Scrip (GRC)

In this fantasy world of the future, the GRC gradually evolved
from that part of the global trade that was operated as barter
in the 1990s. It is by now managed by a consortium of global
corporations and is based on a standard basket of key goods
and services so that it is inflation-proof as well as automati-
cally convertible worldwide. It is run in a way that would have
encouraged long-term sustainability. Several other private corporate currencies, or scrips, are also competing on the Net,
issued by such companies as American Express and
Microsoft.

Regional Currencies

Three regional currencies would follow the success of the
Euro dollar, which replaced national currencies in key European countries in 1999; an Asian Yuan Currency zone; and
finally a NAFTA dollar.

National Currencies

A number of countries have not joined a Regional Currency
Treaty, but because of the growth of the cybereconomy and
Internet currencies, even for them the old national currencies
play a gradually diminishing role.

Complementary Currencies

Because of the globalization process, self-organization of
monetary systems at local levels has become quite popular.

The Information Age also meant a systematic reduction of production and service-related "jobs." As jobs got scarcer, communities created their own currencies in order to facilitate local exchanges among their members. Once a critical mass was attained, automatic clearinghouses on the Net made it possible for members of these communities to participate in the cybereconomy as well.

These four basic methods would alter the entire global system for what is, after all, a method of exchange. The method up to 1999 has facilitated greed and scarcity, leaving vast numbers of people on the planet entirely poor, additional very large numbers of people struggling to make ends meet, and just a very few people extremely wealthy—an unbalanced situation at best.

Here is "the urn of gold" that is "found and then restored." Note the way the sentence is put together—it is not that the urn is merely discovered, like some treasure on a remote island, but that it is found and then restored. Put another way, the method to make wealth available is found, then restored to its original place.

2025 CORPORATIONS TAKE OVER

*. . . with good intentions, prudence, and cunning
there will be results and across the world the culture
will change because of it.*[1]

This chapter is concerned with one of the biggest changes we
may see in our future: the rise of corporations to greater
power and wealth than nations. The Net is the most fashion-
able and lucrative invention human nature has ever created,
but in creating it we also created all the potential side effects.
In the above article's scenario, instead of changing internally
to adapt themselves to their newly expanded social role, corporations have reshaped the world to their own priorities.

One of the key driving forces in this scenario is that information is fast becoming the world's key resource. But not all
institutions benefit equally from such a radical change. Government bureaucracies, not troubled by the pressures of competition, have always been slower than the private sector to adapt to
change. Until recently, inefficiency and lagging behind with
innovative technologies didn't have that much impact on effectiveness. But with information technology the speed of change
has reached a much higher level, so a similar technological time
lag now leaves government agencies in the Stone Age.

Although most people are not aware of it, the Information Revolution has already started to change the nature of money as well. For example, frequent-flier miles have grown from a marketing gimmick into a full private exchange facility for everything short of cash itself. At first, airlines only offered cheaper or free flights for miles earned. Now it's possible to use the miles earned from credit card purchases and redeem them for hotels, car rentals, and other discounts. During the new millennium it's likely that air miles will be exchangeable for cash.

A natural expansion of this trend will be that corporations will create their own currencies for use in any form of exchange. Not only governments will lose from this trend toward corporate currencies, as other factors will contribute to a loss of privacy and individual rights in favor of company policies. There will be a greater requirement of identification. The need for personal identification to ensure the security in electronic payments will increase, and this in turn will create the opportunity to trace who buys what, providing corporations with a greater chance to behave like "big brothers." This then provides the chance for large organizations to build full identification of individuals and their private lives and habits.

The other slightly alarming factor in all this future possibility—where, as Nostradamus says, "with good intentions, prudence, and cunning there will be results and across the world the culture will change because of it"—is that good intentions may not be the reality. We could easily find that companies we have never heard of possess more knowledge of our lives and activities than we would wish even our closest relatives to have.

One of the biggest Net companies in the world, for example, Cedant, is almost certainly not known to many of us. And yet this corporation, at the end of the millennium, has psychographic and transaction data on more than 100 million people, roughly half of all American households! It sells more than a million items online and owns many hotel chains and an enormous amount of residential real estate. Just in relation to the mortgage capability of Cedant's subsidiaries it is necessary for applicants to supply all manner of personal and financial details, including medical information, because the applicant needs life insurance to get the mortgage, all of which data then presumably enter the group's overall database. With the purchase of the property come special discounts and benefits from a list of local dining opportunities available through Premier Dining, an affiliated company, and an offer on discount books about the area published by likewise affiliated Entertainment Publications. The group capitalization is in the range of $22 billion. By the early years of the new millennium the group expects to be able to supply up to 95 percent of all U.S. consumers' needs—somewhere in the range of three million types of goods and services.[2]

Estimates of this kind of Net-based business for the years 2007–2025 show that this and similar companies will be capable of servicing more than a trillion dollars of retail business in the United States. Interactive shopping does everything a profitable business dreams of: Basic costs such as communications, database, and hardware go down while prices go up. Small retail businesses will simply disappear in large numbers, replaced by online shopping outlets. Traditional businesses will face bankruptcy or have to turn to the Net for their profits.

Finally, the one of the most vital necessities of this kind of trading is size, because greater discounts are available with greater volume purchases. The Net shopping systems of the future will therefore be in the hands of very few companies—maybe as few as ten altogether in the United States.

And this is to say nothing of the fact that the Internet can just as easily service global needs as it can purely U.S. needs.

Watch out for the new millennium's "big brother" watching you. The fantasy fiction of George Orwell's novel *1984* could easily catch up in the history of the future.

Hell on Earth

As an extension of the economic changes outlined in previous sections of the book, there is one last scenario worth exhibiting—*Hell on Earth*—a common enough picture painted in several of the prophecies that derive from Nostradamus's predictions—so much so that another verse from his *Centuries* does not seem necessary.

The seedbed for *Hell on Earth* is a combination of breakdowns. In *Hell on Earth* instead of people organizing themselves in self-contained communities, a highly individualistic "free-for-all" ensues. It is the world that would result if enough people believe that the solution to any breakdown is to buy more bullets for their guns.

In this scenario, in *Hell on Earth* everybody is real, actually existing early in this new century. The lives of Red, Sean, Addison, Tod, and Jeremy are described in the words of an interviewer with whom the idea was tested and reported in the book *The Future of Money*,[3] as mentioned in other parts of this text. What we learn is that *Hell on Earth* is *already* happening. And it is only a quarter of an hour's drive away from the wealthiest counties and the fastest growing economies in the United States. *Hell on Earth* is happening in the backyard of the world's only superpower and most advanced technological innovator. It is happening during one of the longest economic boom periods on record, during a time when the Dow Jones has broken its record high more than forty times.

The linkage between this situation and our topic of money may appear obvious: joblessness, bankruptcy, and/or financial failure has made the parents of these kids lose their homes in the first place. Once started, the currency scarcity snowball continues: without an education there is no way that these kids will get a job. There will not even be money for their burial.

Mental illness seems to be another way out: a Chicago study found that 32.2 percent of newly admitted mental patients had a history of homelessness prior to their first hospitalization.[4]

Hell on Earth describes a world where there is a lot of work to be done, but there is simply no money around to bring the people and the work together. It becomes a way of life when children have no chance to develop whatever talents they may have, guaranteeing that the situation will perpetuate, possibly for generations.

It has proven remarkably difficult to find reliable statistics about homelessness and particularly homeless children in America. As one apologetic data administrator put it: "People who have the money are not interested in finding out; those who are interested don't have the money to find out. And researchers do the studies for which they can get paid." She explained that the best data are generated indirectly, because each county keeps track of actual numbers of families and children who seek assistance and are eligible for a particular shelter program (the AFDC-HAP) during each fiscal year. These numbers reflect by definition only "eligible recipients," so the actual numbers have to be higher.[5]

There may be many reasons why the parents of these children became homeless, but the simplest is straightforward arithmetic. The average household income in the California Bay Area increased by 34.3 percent between 1980 and 1990. The cost of living went up during that time by 64 percent, almost double that amount. The average rent for a two-bedroom unit increased by 110 percent over the same time period, while a vacant studio rent increased by a whopping 288 percent. This explains why 20 percent of the homeless families have at least one parent with a full-time job. In short, the fastest rising component of the homeless is simply the families of "working poor" of the past.[6]

Nor should one surmise that San Francisco is somehow a strange anomaly. Because the U.S. Department of Education funds a project tracking schooling problems experienced by homeless children, it has prepared a Report for the U.S. Congress identifying the different ages of homeless children. Here again, only eligible recipients are counted, which means these children still have to be enough "in the system" to actually try to go to school. The most striking aspect of these statistics is the dramatic increase of homeless children in the lowest age brackets (less than six years old).

"Trickle-down theory" or "hoping for better economic times" is clearly not addressing the problem. In parallel, the number of families getting federal housing help dropped from 400,000 in the 1970s to 40,000 in the Reagan years (mid-1980s) to 0 after the National Housing Act passed in September 1996.[7]

Forecasts, which are available only for certain cities, are even worse. New York City, for instance, expects the number of homeless families identified at shelters to multiply by a factor of five between now and the year 2005 because of the dismantling of the federal social security network.

Having a full-time job at minimum wage does not provide someone a home anywhere in America. In 1996, the U.S. Conference of Mayors found that nationwide 19 percent of the homeless population was employed. Declining wages have put housing out of reach of many workers: in no state can a full-time minimum wage earner afford the costs of a one-bedroom unit at fair market rent. In forty-five states and the District of Columbia, families would need to earn at least double the minimum wage in order to afford a two-bedroom apartment at fair market prices. The fastest-growing segment of the homeless population is families with children: they constitute now about 40 percent of people who become homeless. Requests for emergency shelter by families with children in twenty-nine U.S. cities are increasing at the rate of 7 percent per year. The same study found that 24 percent of the requests for shelter by homeless families were being denied owing to lack of resources. The net result: children now account for 27 percent of the total homeless population, and their age has been dropping systematically. While in 1987 the average age of a homeless child in New York City was nine years, now it is down to four years. This average has been dropping notwithstanding the appearance of another new type of homeless New Yorker:

the homeless college student.[8] In 1986 the chancellor of CUNY (City University of New York) estimated that about 3,000 of the students enrolled in his programs were in fact homeless.[9] One of these students was perplexed to discover the United Nations Charter of Universal Human Rights, which the United States has officially signed and keeps referring to in international political debates. However, Congress has not yet approved that treaty because it includes as fundamental the "right for adequate shelter and education."[10]

All this is happening *before* the transfer of the responsibility of the U.S. welfare system to the states and municipalities decided in 1996. According to the Children's Defense Fund of Washington, D.C., the current welfare reform will throw an additional 1 million children into poverty.[11] The only real solution to welfare is jobs, and jobs in the Information Age are definitely not for the "laggards" now defined as those who cannot grasp the latest in information technologies. Furthermore, there are no minimum standards for local welfare. Therefore, it is predictable that there will be competition toward the lowest common denominator (otherwise, there will be mass migration toward the areas with more generous welfare support). This "beggar thy neighbor" game has already started: New Orleans and Atlanta have made it illegal to sleep in the streets, so where will the homeless people from that area go, except to the better-funded remaining social shelters until they become overrun.[12] To compound the problem, states and cities are now under a mandatory balanced-budget requirement, so when the next recession hits they will all have to cut back their social programs exactly when they are needed the most.

Finally, for those who believe that all this could not possibly be relevant for them under any circumstances, there are some sobering reality checks in terms of the historically unprecedented growth in financial risks for the U.S. middle class. Most middle-class savings have been moved from the relatively risk-free bonds to mutual funds and stocks (stock-holders have increased from 12 million to 45 million in the past ten years).[13] This move is the fundamental force that has created the biggest bull stock market in history. However, this also means that these savings are now invested under a significantly higher risk level than ever before.

A dollar meltdown—with its direct impact on the stock market—would hit the broad American public exactly when and where it hurts most, just after the last shreds of the safety net concocted under the New Deal have been dismantled.

Hell on Earth would spread the effects of what is occasionally referred to as "inevitable Social Darwinism" from a minority today to a larger part of the population by 2020.

CONCLUSION

> *He or she who is intelligent can learn from my pre-*
> *dictions that it is possible to discover the correct*
> *path to take, as if there were footprints in the sand*
> *from those who have gone before. Study the history*
> *of previous cultures, the ancient ones who have pro-*
> *vided witness to inner silence, beauty, light and*
> *benediction. Do not follow the ways of the future cul-*
> *tures who only will wish to pass on weapons of*
> *destruction more horrible with every generation.*
> *Such people have become slaves of their own fears*
> *alone.*[1]

Nostradamus may not have seen the detailed aspects of the future that have been laid out briefly in this book, but he apparently did see a lot of the general trends we now can realistically expect in our future. And this volume is made up of only a small number of verses that the author was able to piece together. There are hundreds more stories to tell among more than nine hundred verses, plus the various presages and letters he prepared in the last years of his life. It seems appropriate here, in this Conclusion, to provide what might have been the essence of his understanding of life and the future paths we may create, for it is we who create the future, not some fate or god up there in the heavens: "People will only become more intelligent if they lose their fear of each other and of themselves."

The book has covered a small number of possible future scenarios, some of which occasionally contradict one another, as we have explained. Nostradamus's range of material is so broad and extraordinary that no one has successfully interpreted all of it to any truly accurate effect. Among the hundreds of different interpretations, however, there are some that appear consistent with one another, and these have often resulted in actual events that coincide with the prophecies—such as the deaths of the two Kennedy brothers, the life of Hitler and others, and so forth. Also, it is, of course, virtually impossible to figure out whether a prophecy reflects a time that has past or a time that has yet to come. In so many cases, a verse will be interpreted as meaning something particular in relation to an event in a contemporary present scenario, and then fail to be fulfilled, thus getting used again for another event or interpretation. This could go on and on, leaving behind a trail of failed possibilities. One day, presumably, perhaps as the world comes to an end, all the prophecies will be attributed to events in Nostradamus's future—used up, so to speak, on the truth of the history of the future. Who knows when that will be—perhaps tomorrow, perhaps next year, or next century, or more likely next millennium.

Peter Lorie
California
April 2002 and beyond

BIBLIOGRAPHY

Manuscripts

Nostradamus, Michel. *Les Oracles de Nostradamus, Astrologue, Medicin et Conseiller Ordinaire des Rois Henry II, Francois II et Charles IX.* Le Pelletier Papers, 1867, 40 rue d'Aboukir, Paris, France.

Nostradamus, Michel. *Les Propheties de M. Michel Nostradamus.* Benoist Rigard Papers, 1568, Musee Arbaud, Aix-en-Provence, France.

Nostradamus, Michel. *Les Propheties de M. Nostradamus, Centuries VIII, IX, X.* Benoist Rigard Papers, n.d., Musee Arbaud, Aix-en-Provence, France.

Books

Aburdene, Patricia, and John Naisbitt. *Megatrends for Women.* New York: Villard Books, 1992.

Allen, Hugh Anthony. *Window in Provence.* Boston: n.p., 1943.

Anglund, Jan Walsh. *A Cup of the Sun: A Book of Poems.* Orlando, FL: Harcourt Brace, 1967.

Aquinas, Thomas. *Aquinas's Shorter Summa: Saint Thomas's Own Concise Version of His Summa Theologica.* Manchester, NH: Sophia Institute Press, 2001.

Campbell, Joseph, and Phil Cousineau. *The Hero's Journey.* Rev. ed. New York: HarperCollins, 1999.

Eisler, Riane. *The Chalice and the Blade: Our History, Our Future.* San Francisco: Harper, 1988.

Fitch, Ed. *A Grimoire of Shadows: Witchcraft, Paganism and Magic*. St. Paul, MN: Llewellyn Publications, 1996.

Forman, Henry James. *The Story of Prophecy in the Life of Mankind*. New York: Tudor Publishing, 1940.

French, Marilyn. *Beyond Power: On Women, Men, and Morals*. New York: Summit Books, 1987.

Goodman, Jeffrey. *We Are the Earthquake Generation: Where and When the Catastrophes Will Strike*. New York: Seaview Books, 1978.

Grady, Sean M. *Plate Tectonics: Earth's Shifting Crust*. San Diego, CA: Lucent Books, 1991.

Greene, Brian. *The Elegant Universe: Superstitions, Hidden Dimensions, and the Quest for the Ultimate Theory*. New York: Vintage Books, 2000.

Jamblichus. *Jamblichus on the Mysteries of the Egyptians, Chaldeans, and Assyrians*. Translated by Thomas Taylor. San Diego, CA: Wizards Bookshelf, 1984.

Kirkpatrick, Sidney. *Edgar Cayce: An American Prophet*. New York: Riverhead Books, 2000.

Kurzweil, Ray. *The Age of the Spiritual Machine: When Computers Exceed Human Intelligence*. New York: Viking, 1999.

Laver, James. *Nostradamus: The Future Foretold*. London: Penguin Books, 1942.

Leoni, Edgar. *Nostradamus, Life and Literature*. New York: Exposition Press, 1961. Reissued as *Nostradamus and His Prophecies*. New York: Bell Publishing, 1982.

Lietaer, Bernard. *The Future of Money*. London: Century Publishing.

Lorie, Peter, and Liz Greene. *Nostradamus: The Millennium and Beyond*. New York: Simon & Schuster, 1993.

Lovelock, James, and Lewis Thomas. *The Ages of Gaia: A Biography of Our Living Earth*. New York: Norton & Company, 1988.

O'Conner, Edward. *Marian Apparitions Today-Why S*. N.p., 1996.

Park, Ken. *The World Almanac and Book of Facts 2002*. New York: World Almanac Education, 2001.

Schaar, John H. *Legitimacy in the Modern State*. Reprint ed. New Brunswick, NJ: Transaction Books, 1989.

Sheldrake, Rupert. *A New Science of Life: The Hypothesis of Morphic Resonance*. Rochester, VT: Park Street Press, 1995.

Sjöö, Monica, and Barbara Mor. *The Great Cosmic Mother: Rediscovering the Religion of the Earth*. 2d ed. San Francisco: Harper, 1991.

Tertullian. *Treatises on Penance: On Penitence and on Purity*. Translated by William P. Le Saint. Westminster, MD: Newman Press, 1959.

Wolf, Naomi. *Fire with Fire: The New Female Power and How to Use It*. New York: Random House, 1993.

World Commission on Environment and Development. *Our Common Future*. Oxford: Oxford University Press, 1987.

Web Sites

Berkeley Orthopaedic Biomechanics, Univ. of Cal. at Berkeley [online] http://biomech2.me.berkeley.edu.

Cedant Web Hosting, Cedant, Inc. [online] http://www.cedant.com.

Center for Disease Control, National Center for HIV, STD and TB Prevention [online] http://www.cdc.gov/hiv/stats.htm.

Changing the Scale of the Traditional City, Ball State University [online] http://publish.bsu.edu/perera/Exhibition/images/05moskau.pdf&e=543.

Col. Gadhafi and Libyan Government, John McCartney [online] http://www.geocities.com/libyapage/gadhafi.htm.

Ecology Action, Ecology Action group [online] http://www.growbiointensive.org.

Francisco Varela's Home Page, Francisco Varela, National Institute for Scientific Research, Salpêtrière Univ. Hosp., Paris [online] http://web.ccr.jussieu.fr/varela.

The Library of Economics and Liberty, Liberty Fund [online] http://www.econlib.org/Malthus/malPlog.html.

NASA Academy of Program and Project Leadership, NASA [online] http://appl.nasa.gov/knowledge/issues/isues_articles_intel_arch/html.

New Bone from Scratch! Synthetic Matrix!, John Davies, Univ. of Toronto [online] http://www.dochemp.com/newbone.html.

Priests (Ordination of Women) Measure, Anglican Church, UK [online] http://www.hmso.gov.uk/measures/Ukcm_19930002_en_1.htm.

Religious Tolerance, About, Alternative Religions [online] http://www.religioustolerance.org/rajneesh.htm.

E. Schroedinger, "Schroedinger's Cat" [online] http://www.acyone.com/max/physics/laws/s.html.

Scripps Institution of Oceanography, Univ. of Cal. at San Diego [online] http://scrippsnews.ucsd.edu/pressreleases/Keelingtides.html.

State of the World Population, 1999, United Nations Population Fund [online] http://www.unfpa.org/swp/spmain.htm.

Time, Time, Inc. [online] http://www.time.com/time/time100/builder/profile/watson.html.

Turkish Daily News, 14 December 1996 [online] http://www.turkishdailynews.com/old_editions/12_15_96/feature.htm.

Wetlands Water Resources Programme, World Conservation Union [online] http://www.iisd.ca/sd/iucn/wcc2/sduo139num7.html.

Women's Ministries, Episcopal Church, USA [online] http://www.episcopalchurch.org/2001-334.html.

ENDNOTES

Introduction

1. John H. Schaar, *Legitimacy in the Modern State*, reprint ed. (New York: Transaction Books, 1989), 81–82.

2. Michel Nostradamus, *Les Propheties de M. Michel Nostradamus* (Benoist Rigard Papers, 1568, Musee Arbaud, Aix-en-Provence, France); and Michel Nostradamus, *Les Propheties de M. Nostradamus, Centuries VIII, IX, X* (Benoist Rigard Papers, Musee Arbaud, Aix-en-Provence, France).

3. Jamblichus, *Jamblichus on the Mysteries of the Egyptians, Chaldeans, and Assyrians*, trans. Thomas Taylor (San Diego, CA: Wizards Bookshelf, 1984).

4. The Book of Revelation, by St. John the Divine, is the last book of the New Testament.

5. *The Complete Oxford English Dictionary*, 2d ed., s,v, "mysterium."

6. The confrontation between the American naval fleet and the forces of Colonel Khaddafi of Libya in 1986 was considered a close call for a U.S. war against the Middle East. Matters were concluded when the Libyan dictator backed down.

7. Libyan dictator Mohamar Khaddafi. By some reports, revolutionary Leader Col. Mu`ammar Abu Minyar al-Khaddafi was born in Misurata, Libya, in 1942. Khaddafi led the bloodless military coup against the monarchy of former King Idriss I—Emir Sayyid Mohammed Idriss el-Mahdi el-Senussi. Idriss remained in exile until his death on May 25, 1983, in Cairo. Idriss, born March 13, 1890, in Jarabub, Cyrenaica, became king when Libya gained its independence in 1951. Khaddafi has been chief of state in Libya since 1 September 1969, and became president of Libya in 1977. *Col. Gadhafi and Libyan*

Government, John McCartney [online] http://www.geocities.com/libyapage/gadhafi.htm.

8. Many of Nostradamus's verses contain dating, mostly through astrological references, but few of the successful ones have been totally accurate to the day.

9. Epistle to Henry II, in Nostradamus, *Les Propheties*; and Nostradamus, *Centuries VIII, IX, X*.

September 11, 2001

1. Nostradamus, *Les Propheties*; and Nostradamus, *Centuries VIII, IX, X*.

2. The Huns were a very primitive, warlike group that invaded Europe and caused the defeat and fall of Rome in A.D. 378. They were led by the legendary Attila the Hun.

3. "The King of Angoulmois" was Duke Angouleme (or Angoulmois) of France, also King Francis II.

The Prophecies—Old and Young

2003: GLOBAL ECONOMIES

1. Nostradamus, *Les Propheties*; and Nostradamus, *Centuries VIII, IX, X*.

2. Bernard Lietaer, *The Future of Money* (London: Century Publishing).

3. Ibid.

4. Ibid.

5. Ibid.

6. Bernard Lietaer is a Belgian economist currently working in Europe and the United States.

7. Lietaer, *The Future of Money*.

8. The habit of hoarding currency ultimately affects the flow of currency in any one region, thus reducing the chances of those in poverty from gaining access to it.

2003: SUSTAINING AN ABUNDANT FUTURE

1. Nostradamus, *Les Propheties*; and Nostradamus, *Centuries VIII, IX, X*.

2. World Commission on Environment and Development, *Our Common Future* (Oxford: Oxford University Press, 1987), 40–42.

3. Lietaer, *The Future of Money.*

4. Ibid.

2003: THE THIRD ANTICHRIST

1. Nostradamus, *Les Propheties*; and Nostradamus, *Centuries VIII, IX, X.*

2003: EXTINCTION, OVERPOPULATION, FAMINE, AND CLIMATE

1. Nostradamus, *Les Propheties*; and Nostradamus, *Centuries VIII, IX, X.*

2. *Wetlands Water Resources Programme*, World Conservation Union [online] http://www. iisd.ca/sd/iucn/wcc2/sduo139num7.html.

3. *State of the World Population*, 1999, United Nations Population Fund [online] http://www.unfpa.org/swp/spmain.htm.

4. *Ecology Action*, Ecology Action group [online] http://www.growbiointensive. org.

5. Nostradamus, *Les Propheties*; and Nostradamus, *Centuries VIII, IX, X.*

6. Lietaer, *The Future of Money.*

7. Scripps Institution of Oceanography, Univ. of Cal. at San Diego [online] http://scrippsnews.ucsd.edu/pressreleases/Keelingtides. html.

8. Lietaer, *The Future of Money.*

9. Ibid.

10. Ibid.

11. Ibid.

12. Ibid.

2004: THE UNITED STATES OF AMERICA

1. Nostradamus, *Les Propheties*; and Nostradamus, *Centuries VIII, IX, X.*

2. Nostradamus, *Les Propheties*; and Nostradamus, *Centuries VIII, IX, X.*

2005: THE SCIENCE OF SPACE AND TIME

1. Nostradamus, *Les Propheties*; and Nostradamus, *Centuries VIII, IX, X.*

2. Brian Greene, *The Elegant Universe: Superstitions, Hidden Dimensions,*

and the Quest for the Ultimate Theory (New York: Vintage Books, 2000), 128–130.

3. Ibid.

2005: THE NEW WORLD ORDER: THE FUTURE OF CHINA

1. Nostradamus, *Les Propheties*; and Nostradamus, *Centuries VIII, IX, X*.

2. Nostradamus, *Les Propheties*; and Nostradamus, *Centuries VIII, IX, X*.

3. Nostradamus, *Les Propheties*; and Nostradamus, *Centuries VIII, IX, X*.

4. *Encyclopedia Britannica*, s.v. "People's Republic of China" [CD-Rom, 2001].

2005: THE NEW WORLD OLDER AND OLDER AND OLDER

1. Nostradamus, *Les Propheties*; and Nostradamus, *Centuries VIII, IX, X*.

2. Nostradamus, *Les Propheties*; and Nostradamus, *Centuries VIII, IX, X*.

3. *Berkeley Orthopaedic Biomechanics*, Univ. of Cal. at Berkeley [online] http://biomech2.me.berkeley.edu.

4. *New Bone from Scratch! Synthetic Matrix!*, John Davies, Univ. of Toronto [online] http://www.dochemp.com/newbone.html.

2006: ROMAN CATHOLICISM, WORLD GOVERNMENT, AND THE NEW CONTINENT

1. Nostradamus, *Les Propheties*; and Nostradamus, *Centuries VIII, IX, X*.

2. Chavigny worked as an assistant to Nostradamus in compiling and editing his predictions.

2007: THE EARTH'S APOCALYPSE

1. Nostradamus, *Les Propheties*; and Nostradamus, *Centuries VIII, IX, X*.

2. Nostradamus, *Les Propheties*; and Nostradamus, *Centuries VIII, IX, X*.

3. Nostradamus, *Les Propheties*; and Nostradamus, *Centuries VIII, IX, X*.

4. James Lovelock and Lewis Thomas, *The Ages of Gaia, A Biography of Our Living Earth* (New York: Norton & Company, 1988).

5. Several of the best-known prophets and futurists have echoed Nostradamus's predictions in relation to the condition of this planet—including

Edgar Cayce [Sidney Kirkpatrick, *Edgar Cayce, An American Prophet*, reissue ed.] (New York: Riverhead Books, 2001).

6. Lietaer, *The Future of Money*.

7. Jeffrey Goodman, *We Are the Earthquake Generation: Where and When the Catastrophes Will Strike* (New York: Berkley Publishing, 1979), 91–98.

8. Sean Grady, *Plate Tectronics: Earth's Shifting Crust* (San Diego, CA: Lucent Books, 1991).

2008: WOMEN AND POWER

1. Nostradamus, *Les Propheties*; and Nostradamus, *Centuries VIII, IX, X*.

2. Nostradamus, *Les Propheties*; and Nostradamus, *Centuries VIII, IX, X*.

3. Tertullian, *Treatises on Penance: On Penitence and on Purity*, trans. William P. Le Saint (Westminster, MD: Newman Press, 1959). Thomas Aquinas. *Aquinas's Shorter Summa: Saint Thomas's Own Concise Version of His Summa Theologica* (Manchester, NH: Sophia Institute Press, 2001).

4. See, E. Schroedinger, "Schroedinger's Cat" [online] http://www.acyone.com/max/physics/laws/s.html.

5. Patricia Aburdene and John Naisbitt, *Megatrends for Women* (New York: Villard Books, 1992), 61–66.

6. Lietaer, *The Future of Money*.

7. Nostradamus, *Les Propheties*; and Nostradamus, *Centuries VIII, IX, X*.

8. Peter Lorie and Liz Greene, *Nostradamus: The Millennium and Beyond* (New York: Simon & Schuster, 1991).

9. Edgar Leoni, *Nostradamus, Life and Literature* (New York: Exposition Press, 1961), reissued as *Nostradamus and His Prophecies* (New York: Bell Publishing, 1982).

10. Hugh Anthony Allen, *Window in Provence* (Boston: n.p., 1943).

11. Chiron, anagram used by Nostradamus to indicate Henry II of France.

12. *Encyclopedia Brittanica*, s.v. "Deucalion," [CD-Rom, 2001].

13. *Encyclopedia Brittanica*, s.v. "Phaethon," [CD-Rom, 2001].

2009: WOMEN AT THE TOP

1. Nostradamus, *Les Propheties*; and Nostradamus, *Centuries VIII, IX, X*.

2. Monica Sjöö and Barbara Mor, *The Great Cosmic Mother: Rediscovering*

the Religion of the Earth, 2nd ed. (San Francisco: Harper, 1991).

3. Aburdene, *Megatrends for Women*.

4. Ibid.

5. Ibid.

6. Tony Blair, UK Prime Minister at time of writing.

7. Naomi Wolf, *Fire with Fire: The New Female Power and How to Use It* (New York: Random House, 1993).

8. Paul Keating, Prime Minister of Australia 1991–1996.

9. Aburdene, *Megatrends for Women*.

10. Edward O'Conner, *Marian Apparitions Today–Why S* (n.p., 1996).

11. Riane Eisler, *The Chalice and the Blade: Our History, Our Future* (San Francisco: Harper, 1988).

12. Ibid.

13. Ibid.

14. Joseph Campbell, and Phil Cousineau, *The Hero's Journey*, rev. ed. (New York: HarperCollins, 1999).

15. *Turkish Daily News*, 14 December 1996, [online] http://www. turkishdailynews.com/old_editions/12_15_96/feature.htm.

16. Nostradamus, *Les Propheties*; and Nostradamus, *Centuries VIII, IX, X*.

17. *Priests (Ordination of Women) Measure*, Anglican Church, UK [online] http://www.hmso.gov.uk/measures/Ukcm_19930002_en_1.htm.

18. Aburdene, *Megatrends for Women*.

19. Ibid.

20. *Women's Ministries*, Episcopal Church, USA [online] http://www. episcopalchurch.org/2001-334.html.

21. Aburdene, *Megatrends for Women*.

22. Nostradamus, *Les Propheties*; and Nostradamus, *Centuries VIII, IX, X*.

23. Aburdene, *Megatrends for Women*.

24. Ibid.

25. *Francisco Varela's Home Page*, Francisco Varela, National Institute for Scientific Research, Salpêtière Univ. Hosp., Paris [online] http:// web.ccr.jussieu.fr/varela.

26. *Religious Tolerance*, About, Alternative Religions [online] http:// www.religioustolerance.org/rajneesh.htm.

27. Rupert Sheldrake, *A New Science of Life: The Hypothesis of Morphic Resonance* (Rochester, VT: Park Street Press, 1995).

28. Ed Fitch, *A Grimoire of Shadows: Witchcraft, Paganism and Magic* (St. Paul, MN: Llewellyn Publications, 1996).

29. Nostradamus, *Les Propheties*; and Nostradamus, *Centuries VIII, IX, X.*

30. Nostradamus, *Les Propheties*; and Nostradamus, *Centuries VIII, IX, X.*

31. César, son of Nostradamus.

32. Michel Nostradamus, *Les Oracles de Nostradamus, astrologue, medicin et conseiller ordinaire des rois Henry II, Francois II et Charles IX* (Le Pelletier Papers, 1867, 40 rue d'Aboukir, Paris, France).

33. Peter Lorie and Liz Greene, *Nostradamus: The Millennium and Beyond* (New York: Simon & Schuster, 1991).

34. *The Complete Oxford English Dictionary*, 2d. ed., s.v. "an."

35. Nostradamus, *Les Propheties*; and Nostradamus, *Centuries VIII, IX, X.*

36. Nostradamus, *Les Propheties*; and Nostradamus, *Centuries VIII, IX, X.*

37. Eisler, *The Chalice and the Blade.*

38. Marilyn French, *Beyond Power: On Women, Men, and Morals* (New York: Summit Books, 1987).

39. Aburdene, *Megatrends for Women.*

40. Naomi Wolf, *Fire with Fire: The New Female Power and How to Use It* (New York: Random House, 1993).

41. Jan Walsh Anglund, *A Cup of the Sun: A Book of Poems* (New York: Harcourt Brace; 1967).

42. Leoni, *Nostradamus, Life and Literature.*

43. Ibid.

44. Ibid.

45. Ibid.

2009: FAMILY FORTUNES

1. Nostradamus, *Les Propheties*; and Nostradamus, *Centuries VIII, IX, X.*

2. Ken Park, *The World Almanac and Book of Facts 2002* (New York: World Almanac Education, 2001).

3. *Changing the Scale of the Traditional City*, Ball State University [online] http://publish.bsu.edu/perera/Exhibition/images/05moskau.pdf&e=543.

2009: COMPUTERS AND THE INTERNET: FASTER AND FASTER AND FASTER

1. Nostradamus, *Les Propheties*; and Nostradamus, *Centuries VIII, IX, X*.
2. Nostradamus, *Les Propheties*; and Nostradamus, *Centuries VIII, IX, X*.
3. *Time*, Time, Inc. [online] http://www.time.com/time/time100/builder/profile/watson. html.
4. Ray Kurzweil, *The Age of the Spiritual Machine: When Computers Exceed Human Intelligence* (New York: Viking, 1999).
5. Ibid.
6. Ibid.
7. Ibid.
8. Ibid.
9. Ibid.
10. Ibid.
11. Ibid.
12. Ibid.

2010: THE END OF FEAR

1. Nostradamus, *Les Propheties*; and Nostradamus, *Centuries VIII, IX, X*.

2011: ANIMALS AND CHIPS

1. Nostradamus, *Les Propheties*; and Nostradamus, *Centuries VIII, IX, X*.
2. *NASA Academy of Program and Project Leadership*, NASA [online] http://appl.nasa.gov/knowledge/issues/isues_articles_intel_arch/html.

2012: HOW MANY HUMANS?

1. Nostradamus, *Les Propheties*; and Nostradamus, *Centuries VIII, IX, X*.
2. Park, *World Almanac*.
3. Thomas Robert Malthusin in *The Library of Economics and Liberty*, Liberty Fund [online] http://www.econlib.org/Malthus/malPlog.html.
4. Park, *World Almanac*.
5. Ibid.
6. Ibid.
7. Nostradamus, *Les Propheties*; and Nostradamus, *Centuries VIII, IX, X*.

8. Nostradamus, *Les Propheties*; and Nostradamus, *Centuries VIII, IX, X.*
9. Nostradamus, *Les Propheties*; and Nostradamus, *Centuries VIII, IX, X.*

2013–2014: THE EARLY 2000s—AIDS, FULL REALIZATION
1. Epistle to Henry II in Nostradamus, *Les Propheties*; and Nostradamus, *Centuries VIII, IX, X.*
2. Nostradamus, *Les Propheties*; and Nostradamus, *Centuries VIII, IX, X.*
3. *Center for Disease Control*, National Center for HIV, STD and TB Prevention [online] http://www.cdc.gov/hiv/stats.htm.
4. Ibid.

2015: THE END OF DEPRESSION
1. Nostradamus, *Les Propheties*; and Nostradamus, *Centuries VIII, IX, X.*

2016–2020: THE GOLDEN AGE
1. Epistle to Henry II in Nostradamus, *Les Propheties*; and Nostradamus, *Centuries VIII, IX, X.*
2. Nostradamus's letter to his son César in Nostradamus, *Les Propheties*; and Nostradamus, *Centuries VIII, IX, X.*

2020–2025: HOW MONEY MIGHT BE
1. Nostradamus, *Les Propheties*; and Nostradamus, *Centuries VIII, IX, X.*
2. Lietaer, *The Future of Money.*

2025: CORPORATIONS TAKE OVER
1. Nostradamus, *Les Propheties*; and Nostradamus, *Centuries VIII, IX, X.*
2. *Cedant Web Hosting*, Cedant, Inc. [online] http://www.cedant.com.
3. Lietaer, *The Future of Money.*
4. Ibid.
5. Ibid.
6. *State of the World Population*, 1999 [online].
7. Ibid.
8. Ibid.

9. Chancellor of CUNY, City University of New York, 1986.

10. *State of the World Population*, 1999 [online].

11. Ibid.

12. Ibid.

13. Ibid.

CONCLUSION

1. Nostradamus, *Les Propheties*; and Nostradamus, *Centuries VIII, IX, X*.